Selected Papers from the Asia Conference on Economics & Business Research 2015

Stanley Soh
Editor

Selected Papers from the Asia Conference on Economics & Business Research 2015

Springer

Editor
Stanley Soh
Aventis School of Management
Singapore
Singapore

ISBN 978-981-10-0985-3 ISBN 978-981-10-0986-0 (eBook)
DOI 10.1007/978-981-10-0986-0

Library of Congress Control Number: 2016937947

Printed on acid-free paper

This Springer imprint is published by Springer Nature
The registered company is Springer Science+Business Media Singapore Pte Ltd.

Preface

The 2015 Asia Conference on Economics & Business Research (ACEB) organised by Aventis School of Management, Asia's Leading Graduate School, was held during 18–19 November 2015 in Concorde Hotel Singapore. ACEB aims to bring together leading scholars, students and practitioners from Asia and the rest of the world for an academic exchange. The goal of ACEB is to create opportunities for international research collaborations, scientific information interchange and facilitate relationship building in the Economics and Business disciplines.

The conference consisted of two one-hour plenary lectures by Mr. Richard Jerram, Chief Economist, Bank of Singapore and Prof. Eiji Ogawa, Faculty of International Finance at Graduate School of Commerce and Management, Hitotsubashi University, Japan.

A total of 62 registered delegates from the following countries and regions, namely Singapore, Pakistan, Oman, Philippines, India, Korea, United Kingdom, Hong Kong, Australia, USA, South Africa, Indonesia, Thailand, Mexico, Malaysia, China, participated in ACEB 2015.

Participants were invited to submit papers to the present volume. We wish to thank both Mr. Stanley Goh, Academic Director of Aventis School of Management and Ms. Vivian Li, Conference Manager of Asia Pacific International Academy for coordinating the reviewing of the submitted papers.

Asia Pacific International Academy (APIA)

Asia Pacific International Academy (APIA), a subsidiary of Aventis School of Management, was founded in 2010 with the purpose of promoting academic research and intellectual development of researchers, academicians and professionals from various institutions and across different countries in the Asia-Pacific region and beyond through academic conferences and executive training.

Aventis School of Management

Aventis School of Management is a Leading Graduate School dedicated to the development of professional and business leaders. Aventis is a member of the European Foundation for Management Development (EFMD), European Council for Business Education (ECBE), Executive MBA Council and United Nations (UN) Global Compact partnership. Through our close collaboration with professional bodies, including the Chartered Institute of Marketing (CIM UK) and American Association for Financial Management (AAFM), Aventis qualifications are industry-driven and recognised by professional bodies internationally.

ACEB Officers

Samuel Teo
General Manager
Aventis School of Management, Singapore
E-mail: samuel@aventisglobal.edu.sg

Stanley Soh
Academic Director
Aventis School of Management, Singapore
E-mail: Stanley@aventisglobal.edu.sg

Vivian Li
Conference Manager
Asia Pacific International Academy, Singapore
E-mail: vivian@aventisglobal.edu.sg

Contents

Mexican Entrepreneurial Culture as a Key Factor of Success for Micro, Small, and Medium Enterprises

José G. Vargas-Hernández and Mauro Francisco Alatorre Villarruel

Abstract This paper aims to devise a personal dissertation about the impact of the culture in the Mexican Entrepreneur as a key factor that determines the performance of Companies/Business, what for its sizes are classified as SMEs, this personal dissertation is developed through the analysis of several articles published by diverse authors which address the cultural aspect inside of the organization.

Keywords Corporate culture · Family business · Entrepreneur · Mexico · SMEs

JEL M140 · L250 · L260

1 Introduction

The current research paper starts from an aspect of personal motivation because it is deeply connected with the research object which at the moment is being conducting. Therefore, this paper intends to present, from a general perspective, the impact of cultural factors on the development, growth, and continuity of Mexican companies.

Mexico is a country that is characterized by its high melting pot of cultures present in each of the regions that comprise it. In this situation, a vast variety of individuals who share a set of traditions and customs inherited, and where it is present the cultural influence from civilizations of pre-Columbian times as well as the influence of beliefs, codes and Spanish institutions set up during the colonial era which were from the European, such as the Catholic religion.

J.G. Vargas-Hernández (✉) · M.F.A. Villarruel
University Center for Economic and Managerial Sciences,
University of Guadalajara, Periférico Norte 799 Edif. G.201-7,
Núcleo Universitario Los Belenes, 45100 Zapopan, Jalisco, Mexico
e-mail: jvargas2006@gmail.com; jgvh0811@yahoo.com; josevargas@cucea.udg.mx

S. Soh (ed.), *Selected Papers from the Asia Conference on Economics & Business Research 2015*, DOI 10.1007/978-981-10-0986-0_1

While these cultural beliefs are shared in some degree of similarity with other Spanish-speaking countries of Latin America as different continents, it is clear that society forming a national identity is not such because the individuals in each region are subject to environmental conditions that differ completely from latitude to latitude, thereby generating a disparity in the ability of individuals to access various elements or information of their environment. Based on these settings, individuals begin to build and adapt informal institutions that have as their formative and cognitive pillars (Scott 1995), giving as a result, the introduction of behaviors that make individuals in society.

It should be noted, as distinguished Peng (2012) that established institutions by individuals play an important role in the conditions of performance of organizations involved as a positive or negative effect on their prosperity.

Following the changes in recent decades, these institutions have gained greater importance in the development of business activities of economic agents, becoming a key element to achieve competitiveness and retention of businesses. Businesses now not only participate in a purely local environment but also are challenged by foreign organizations from an increasingly internationalized world, where only those with an entrepreneurial spirit and initiative leverage best business opportunities from the market. Therefore in the XXI century, it becomes essential to achieve an intellectual revolution that sets new basis for achieving a full renewal of institutions and organizations in order to adapt to the requirements of the new millennium.

In the case of Mexico, this transition takes on a new urgency as a result of serious cultural gaps possessed by individuals, specifically entrepreneurs. Entrepreneurs tend to move toward an essentially conservative and paternalistic perspective rather than an entrepreneurial orientation of liberal principles, proceeding to spread through generations of behaviors that threaten the good organizational practice within companies. This practice leads to refer the behavior of an individual, the employer, affecting the progress of the organization because its actions mark strategic and tactical direction in the operations of the company.

Therefore, this research paper tries to make a judgment, based on a review of previous research from national and Latin American academic institutions focusing on internal corporate culture of SMEs that reflects the real cultural situation of Mexican entrepreneurs. The aim is to show the great impact and importance that lie in those institutional, educational, and cognitive pillars. This, under the vision of raising awareness regarding the need for a single ideological shift, where the relevance of the optimal preparation and fitness initiative focuses on recognition, decision risk, cooperation, trust and innovation, and joint elements that make good use of the opportunities available.

2 Background

Initially, it should be considered that organizations are made up of individuals who are subject to social structures established in the environment, and where they live with the rest of the members that make up their collective and communities. Higuita (2012) defines the organization as a cultural and socio-structural system which generates its own corporate culture based on the ideology of its members who compose it, including individuals who are driven by an entrepreneurial nature of character and they are especially/entrepreneurial, i.e., homeowners or business owners. Vaca et al. (2010) note that maturity; experiences and events lived up personal axes that make up the personality and individual identity.

Such factors have a great importance in understanding the business and the dynamic action of the employer since these bases, as suggested Cow (2010), define the capacity and competence of the entrepreneur's own organizational processes to generate high quality. Likewise, Saavedra and Tapia (2011) indicate as well that among the characteristics that provide greater competitiveness to SMEs are found the experiences, ideas, and aspirations of the employer. By means of which, the inner structure of companies is defined as the scope of strategic management performed by the company, reaffirming the importance of sociocultural aspects in the dynamism and permanence of SMEs because they set the behavior of firms (Saavedra and Tapia 2012).

These institutions can become an obstacle to the development of a high-level competitiveness, adaptability, productivity, and succession of any organization. Rodríguez et al. (2013) suggest that the success of SMEs lies, briefly, on two pillars that serve as cornerstones in the business gestation and perpetuity which are entrepreneurship and innovation capacity because these axes acquire value theoretically coveted enterprise features.

The significance behind the success of SMEs lies in the fact that these economic agents, as noted by Rodríguez et al. (2013), become units of opportunity for developing nations in a long period of time. This is evident due to its large dominance not only in the Mexican market but also internationally, reaching an average value classified as SMEs 85 % worldwide, Out of these, 90 % have a assiduously family character companies (Rodríguez et al. 2013). In the case of Mexico, there are 3.6 million classified companies in that category by having a number of employees smaller than 500 people, representing 99 % of firms in the market and employ 78 % of the workforce economically active existing at local level in the Mexican Republic (INEGI 2009).

While SMEs account for 99 % of organizations in the market, Morales (2011) notes that 65 % of companies in that category disappear in less than two years, of which 50 % goes bankrupt in the first year, generating a result that only 10 % of organizations may survive for a decade. Morales (2011) argues that the corporate mortality rate is so high that only 10 out of 100 companies have a chance to take hold in the market formally. The above event happens on the fact that Mexican businessmen operating under a limited vision focused directly to a temporary short-term period (Saavedra and Tapia 2011). This is added to the culture in Mexican society characterized by sustained would find in relationships where critics are hardly accepted due to the constant struggle to attain a significant degree of authority causing poor teamwork or work commitment (Saavedra and Tapia 2012).

These cultural deficiencies in Mexican society identified by Saavedra and Tapia (2011, 2012) hinder the action of the employer for the formation of processes that leverage internal strengths of the organization and opportunities from the environment to improve its productivity, competitiveness, and survival.

3 Hypothesis

There is a relationship which involves the cultural variable of Mexican society and the level of improvement of micro, small, and medium enterprises (SMEs). Since the entrepreneurial spirit leads the individual on a path of innovation, initiative, cooperation, communication, and risk taking, it depends directly on the beliefs and values which are found dominating the subject, and the organization itself.

4 Research Objectives

This paper has as objectives:

A. To review and analyze various research articles focusing on the topic of corporate culture of SMEs in Mexico, from both national and foreign institutions.
B. To discern, through the analysis of different sources and articles which discussed the possible relationship between the success or failure of companies classified as micro, small, and medium (SME) with the cultural influence behind the Mexican entrepreneur.
C. To develop a personal conclusion from the knowledge found during the preparation of this document that prove or disprove the hypothesis.

5 Research Methodology

The research methodology employed in the process of preparing this research paper is intended for explanatory purposes and leads to a sense of comprehension and understanding of the phenomenon (Vásquez 2005). The research is also descriptive because within its purpose, it identifies ways to conduct or personal attitudes involving potential association of variables under investigation (Vásquez 2005). Such methodological process departs as a result of the analysis of the various empirical, theoretical, and scientific papers that have investigated the cultural factors of Mexican society within firms. These have been used as reference for the implementation and contextualization of the personal ideas expressed in the posterior segments such as judgment or final conclusions.

It should be noted that analyzed research sources come from articles both originated in Mexican and foreign educational institutions, such as publications of the University of Talca in Chile or publications of the Universidad Del Norte in Colombia educational. The use of both local and foreign sources aims to provide a vision and connotation of the potential for economic success that is displayed in small and medium-sized Mexican companies from a cultural aspect. The contributions conducted by researchers participating from inside as well as researchers of the economic environment that have observed from the outside as a means of understanding the Latin American reality, find possible solutions to local conflicts. In layman's terms, this is a knowledge approach based on both sides of a coin.

The literature detailed in this document has been employed under the objective of developing an argument that seeks to argue a strong cultural relationship in the success or failure of small and medium firms. This is conducted under the assumption that the owner and the members participating in the administration that they are influenced by their values, traditions, and customs, such proposals and observations are presented below.

6 Theoretical Framework

This article aims to sustain research from institutional theory, also known as the theory based from the point of view of the institutions. Scott (1995) points out as one of the theoretical schools of greatest impact in the various administrative disciplines in their search to understand the impact of institutions on their behavior, choices, and performance not only of businesses but also of all individuals involved in the work of an organized society. These theoretical current inquires a more promising approach to the production variables that define the benefits earned by organizations in a society because it established a number of action codes.

These codes not only define but also regulate the decisions of all members in a community (Scott 1995). Scott (1995) likewise points out that the theory of institutions seeks to understand the reasons why organizations are acting under the influence from the institutional structures of the environment. Also, how structured institutions are created, reasons why they set a series of codes of conduct and also determine the impact of its actions on the practices of the organizations.

One goal of the theory is to recognize the elements that define an institution. North (1990) defines institutions as "rules" in a society that aim to establish constraints that shape the ways in which humans interact, conditions which require change and the evolution of societies through time to provide various capacities between individuals. While North (1990) adds that the structures established by the institutions tend to reduce uncertainty to regulate human interactions in every feasible operation. Although both organizations and institutions have similar features in their constitution both have discordant purposes since the organizations are seeking to extend their benefits while institutions are seeking the common good.

Institutions affect organizational performance of companies in its sector since its effects are perceived in the way costs are perceived by firms, ranging from production costs to transaction costs, together with technological advances available in the environment where the organization works (North 1990). So that institutions play an important role in the functioning of society as well as the performance and competitiveness of organizations (North and Thomas 1973). Scott (1983) notes that the differences within organizations are mainly related to operations developed by the institutions. These determine the various prototypes of regulatory, normative, and cultural concepts and standards associated with the creation of mechanisms.

These mechanisms seek to maintain order and welfare of all the participants in the environment. If the elements in the environment evolve institutions are required to make progress, the conceptual framework developed within which to comply with the new perspectives available in the society (Scott 1995). In determining the institutional theory as a starting point in the progress of the current research paper, it becomes necessary to introduce the term culture, its components, and scope so that its importance in the company can be understood. Institutional theory establishes culture as an institution of society, which has an informal and is classified by Scott (1995) as both normative and cognitive pillars behind the actions of individuals and businesses.

There are various definitions of culture, one of which is provided by Hofstede (1997) who defines culture as the various collective features that provide a sense of identity to all members belonging to a society which make it easy to distinguish individuals from specific groups. Such characteristics focussed on the degree of equality among individuals, cooperation, adaptability, as well as the existing level of strategic vision in the subjects. From culture, start codes of conduct that influence the decisions of individuals.

One of the first authors to recognize the importance of cultural variable was Schein (1988) who identifies as a specific dimension in driving and developing an organization to participate as a primary resource for the implementation of organizational processes. Further, he indicates that the problems in the business management of the companies have their origins mainly in cultural variables.

The premise established by Schein (1988) part in the sense that each organization has its own culture, which sets specific dimensions that affects the way in which individuals belonging to any community think, feel, and act. The principle defines the organizational vision of the company and its environment and effects, Schein (1988), explains that occasionally they are negative and cause conflict. Vargas-Hernández et al. (2014, p. 46) point out that culture and strategy are similar to centrifugal and centripetal forces that balance the development and transformation of organizations.

Culture present in society is introduced into the organization providing a great influence on the identity and business culture of the firm, establishing, from their internal structures and the behavior of its members, a number of strategies that seek

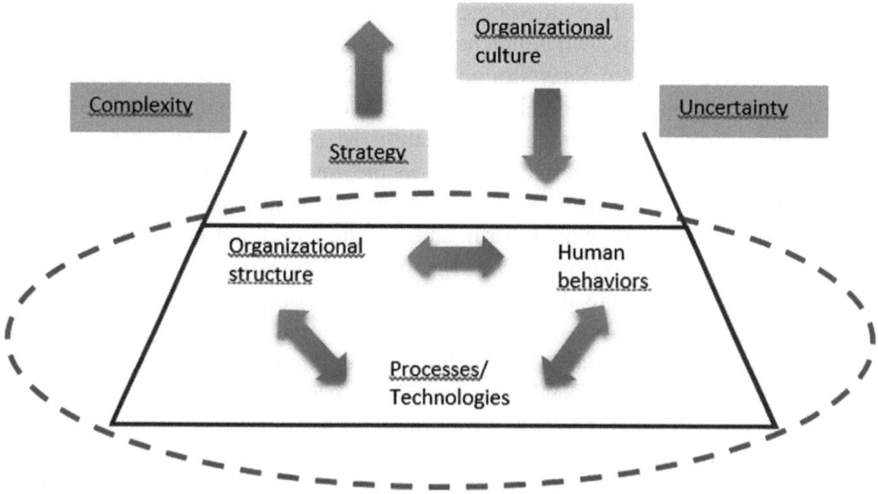

Fig. 1 The interrelationships of organizational culture and strategic in components of modern strategic business model. *Source* Strategic Management Organizations (Vargas-Hernández et al. 2014)

to prevail over the variables of uncertainty and complexity into the environment as evidenced in the Fig. 1 (Vargas-Hernández et al. 2014).

The diagram shows how the culture of society is introduced into the organization in conjunction with the factors and internal structures of firms and corporate-defined actions to combat the uncertainty and complexity of reality strategies.

7 Insight and Analysis of Information

Culture is an institution that establishes the "Rules of the Game" (North 1990) in human societies which demarcate the behavior of individuals and shape a collective identity that allows the association or affiliation of their members in order to achieve related interests. Being organizations or companies, some of the structures are influenced by the presence of the said human institution in their environment.

All human beings are influenced by the culture and the entrepreneur and business man is no exception to the rule, because all development experience throughout their lives. Then this experience is poured in defining the organization, based on their rank according to their own organizational culture which finds members as subjects who are subsequently introduced to the firm. That is, as already noted Higuita (2012), the organization of the culture of their environment is directly represented by the current ideological founder/owner. Departing from this weight and from its own culture within the organization will influence the established culture of its members.

Culture generates culture. Ideological thinking lies behind the Mexican businessman supported by his own deficiencies and strengths in cultural variables in the Mexican society, as stated Saavedra and Tapia (2012). He lists a series of visible behaviors on citizens that generally and directly contradict with desirable characteristics that should be counted for a nation to possess sustainable economic development to ensure collective welfare in the long term. Such desirable traits should be focused on a feeling of moving ahead, take risks, cooperate, adapt, change, innovation, etc., which form an entrepreneurial attitude which can be conceived where the various pillars of organizational development (Rodríguez et al. 2013) are needed to ensure the perpetuation of the companies regardless of their size or the structural conditions of the firm itself.

Morales (2011) notes that 90 % of Mexican companies are classified by their size have a family-owned SMEs status. These organizations have actions and choices that are determined by prevailing family values in Mexican culture, which modify the business vision of owners by providing directions based on the implementation of strategies. This will enable the organization to survive with the minimum necessary conditions to ensure the legacy of the company to its descendants, rather than legitimize the succession of the firm in the long run by creating competitive advantages and productivity (Pérez 2010).

This conflict arises from the owner's inability to distance the family business decisions, inability derived from his cultural values. Gómez and Ricardo (2012) reaffirms that culture defines the performance of organizations arguing that the failure of companies can occur because the culture remains constant and unchanged, even though their environment is constantly changing. Culture, as the institutional structure is, if it does not undergo transformations, cannot generate a welfare state among individuals in a group which leads to a stagnation of economic, technological, and productive sectors (Morales 2011).

While the culture of Mexican society tends to establish organizations with closed integration features, impersonal, dominated by individual short-term needs, where a power struggle and opportunism exhibits, predominantly paternalistic clear vision and conservative ideology originated in the owner. It is possible to establish a paradigm shift in owner's cultural variables. Arias (2004) notes that this is operable through professional training of future entrepreneurs as these tend to integrate all the knowledge acquired in their academic preparation. Further, such teachings changed the vision of their environment, as an example presents the entrepreneurial vision rooted in Monterrey entrepreneurs, thus, making education a key for adaptation element of culture, whereas 50 % of owners do not have optimal studies (Morales 2011).

While the cultural adaptation of a society, such as the Mexican, has a degree of high difficulty in such a way that requires integral structural reform into all institutions and at all levels. It is also true, that the barriers that are imposed by culture can be getting over by the academic preparation of individuals in society (Arias 2004). This can be in conjunction with a behavioral change of the subject, which is only possible with the opening of information from the environment that allows them to understand the need to abandon routines and take advantage of external opportunities being wasted to act under a conservative mentality (Schumpeter 1963). Morales (2011, p. 43) states that intuition is not enough to create a business. To create business it is necessary the professional business training, including organizational capacity, management, and innovation.

It is required a preparation that understands the demands and implications related with establishing an organization where skills strategies generate action that are reflected in the success and perpetuation of the companies. This should be aimed at drawing up to implement a continuum of long-term business projects, to implement a community that accepts all knowledge from the rest of the members of the organization, and by creating connections or networks which can transmit accurate information leading to prudent and feasible elections by senior management (Rodríguez et al. 2013).

To close the current analysis section it should be noted that SMEs, as economic units, are an area of opportunity to generate development in Mexico because of the significant advantages they possess compared to large corporations. Also SMEs are suffering from fewer administration conflicts. Similarly, their size can innovate to create new production processes or introduce new market segments because the cost to implement these strategies require a smaller amount of material, financial, and human resources (Pérez 2010). Only achievable conditions can achieve an institutional transition that breaks with the previously established paradigms whose adaptation goes hand in hand with the environment.

8 Conclusion

The entrepreneur is a rational agent that seeks to achieve its objectives using the means at its disposal from the environment, which is dominated by the relationships and institutions, not only regulatory but also educational and cognitive. One of them, the culture, sets a pattern of collective identity that restricts the behavior, actions, and choices of individuals within the human society.

The way it is structured, the cultural institution determines the effectiveness of the decisions of individuals, including the entrepreneur, who through all patterns of information from his environment and influenced by cultural variables caused by society to which it is subordinated. He sets his own entrepreneurial attitude which in turn provides organizational direction within the firm, sentencing future perpetuation of the company, its success or failure.

The culture of the society can act as a barrier to economic performance not only of business activities but also in the economic performance of a nation, which in turn affects the level of social welfare of individuals (Pérez 2010). These limitations can only be overcome through the educational preparation of a whole generation of future social individuals who can understand the urgent need to generate innovation behind, have initiative of working, group unity and teamwork, where the generation of wealth and authority only result is a superficial consequence to undertake an activity in a competitive, efficient and effective manner.

Citing Rodríguez et al. (2013, p. 790) the most important capital for a country is its people. The entrepreneurial culture as a substantial pillar of the strategic flexibility, it is a relevant, inspiring factor and gives strength to face the attractive challenges in the history and evolution of the company. If the individuals in a society have a poor cultural and academic background, their economic activities will also be deficient.

References

Arias P (2004) Linaje y vicisitudes de la cultura empresarial en Jalisco. Espiral X(30):85–108
Gómez I, Ricardo R (2012) Cultura organizacional: aproximación sectorial en Bogotá. Rev Fac Cien Econ Inv Reflexión XX(2):19–41
Higuita D (2012) Interiorización de las manifestaciones culturales en los miembros de la organización. Rev Fac Cien Econ Inv Reflexión XX(2):127–142
Hofstede G (1997) Cultures and organizations: software of the mind. McGraw Hill, New York
INEGI (2009) Censos Económicos. Instituto Nacional de Estadística y Geografía, México
Morales I (2011) Las pymes en México, entre la creación fallida y la destrucción creadora. Economía Informa, Núm. 366 Enero-Febrero, pp 39–48
North D, Thomas R (1973) The rise of the western world: a new economic history. Cambridge University Press, Cambridge
North D (1990) Institutions, institutional change and economic performance. Cambridge University Press, New York
Peng M (2012) Global strategy. Thompson South-Western, Cincinnati
Pérez, M. (2010). Empresa y familia en México. Una visión desde la antropología, Universidad Iberoamericana, México, 319 p
Rodríguez P, Pico B, Méndez-Ramírez F (2013) Capacidad innovadora en la empresa familiar como área de oportunidad hacia el desarrollo de México. Economía, Sociedad y Territorio, XIII Septiembre-Diciembre, pp 779–794
Saavedra M, Tapia B (2011) Mejores prácticas y factores de competitividad en las micro, pequeñas y medianas empresas mexicanas. Economía 32:11–36
Saavedra M, Tapia B (2012) El Entorno Sociocultural y la Competitividad de la PYME en México. Panorama Socioeconómico, Julio, pp 4–24
Schein E (1988) La cultura empresarial y el liderazgo. Una visión dinámica. Plaza y Janes Editores, Barcelona
Schumpeter J (1963) Teoría del desenvolvimiento económico. Una investigación sobre ganancia, capital, crédito, interés y ciclo económico, 3rd edn. Fondo de Cultura Económica, México
Scott W (1983) Introduction: from technology to environment. In: Organizational environments: ritual and rationality. SAGE, Beverly Hill
Scott W (1995) Institutions and organizations. Sage, Thousand Oaks
Vaca P, Sepúlveda M, Fracica G (2010) Acción del empresario bogotano: creencias y prácticas. Pensamiento & Gestión, Enero-Junio, pp 1–24
Vargas-Hernández J, Guerra E, Bojórquez A, Bojórquez F (2014) Gestión Estratégica de las Organizaciones. Ciudad Autónoma de Buenos Aires: Elaleph.com Ediciones Insumisos Latinoamericanos
Vásquez I (2005) Tipos de Estudios. GestioPolis.com. Recuperado el 11 de 11 de 2009

How Customer Loyalty Represents the Future of Banks: Study of Banking Industry in West Java, Indonesia

Rita Komaladewi, Yuyus Suryana, Budiarto Subroto, Popy Rufaidah and Marthin Nanere

Abstract Free trade is a big challenge for a company to enhance its organization performance. Banking industry also faces challenges because of the free trade, since there have been many companies going bankrupt that it is feared that it will reduce customers' savings or deposits in bank. Competitors needs to be aware because only banks with advantages that are able to create product with high quality services that can satisfy customers. Challenges become harder particularly when customers are sensitive to the interest rate, thus loyalty is at stake. This circumstance is very important because customers define the future of a bank. Having a close relationship between the bank and the customer can become the strength that could increase customer value. The main objective of this research was to study how customer loyalty can be constructed using customer value and relational quality. Data from 178 business customers in 8 banks were collected using questionnaires. Structural Equation Modelling (SEM) was employed based on variance Partial Least Square Path Modeling. The unit of this study was priority customers of banks in West Java, Indonesia. Unlike other studies, the finding suggests that customer relational quality has a dominant contribution to loyalty

---

R. Komaladewi (✉) · Y. Suryana · P. Rufaidah
Department of Management and Business, Universitas Padjadjaran, Bandung, Indonesia
e-mail: rita.komaladewi@fe.unpad.ac.id

Y. Suryana
e-mail: yuyus.suryana@fe.unpad.ac.id

P. Rufaidah
e-mail: popy.rufaidah@fe.unpad.ac.id

B. Subroto
Department of Management, Graduate School of Sahid University, Jakarta, Indonesia
e-mail: budiarto01@yahoo.com

M. Nanere
La Trobe Business School, La Trobe University, Melbourne, Australia
e-mail: m.nanere@latrobe.edu.au

S. Soh (ed.), *Selected Papers from the Asia Conference on Economics & Business Research 2015*, DOI 10.1007/978-981-10-0986-0_2

compared to customer-perceived value. This may be due to the fact that customer relational quality with emotional touch maintained by employees of the bank may have caused customers to be dependent to partnership with the bank.

Keywords Customer-perceived value · Relational quality · Loyalty · Bank · West Java

Contribution of Study Personal relationships between bank's employees and the customer are very important. Customer dependence need to be created. Customers who have been very emotionally attached will feel disloyal when saving their money is saved elsewhere. This is the first study looking at loyalty at the banking sector in West Java.

1 Introduction

One of the key strategies for a bank to be able to maintain both growth and market share in the marketing environment with a high level of competition is the ability of the bank to identify and satisfy both the needs and the wants of customers, better and faster than its competitors. According to Yavas and Babakus (2008), if customers are satisfied with the services of a bank, then customers will save their money in the bank. Customer loyalty is the desired expectation of a company from its customer (Kotler and Keller 2012; Leingpbul et al. 2009). Based on the current condition in which the competition intensifies, banks compete against each other to improve their performance by offering products and services. This may attract customers to choose and remain to be customers of the bank. With the changes in the annual bank rates due to the rise and fall of customer's fund, it has shown that customers have had priority in choosing where to invest or save their money. Fierce competition between banks may cause customers to have the power to determine which bank they wish to choose for their business. In a business like banks, service is a top priority, and customer-oriented banks are the banks that will be selected by customers, and will win the competition. Banks should be customers-oriented, and these customers will help to determine the future of the banks.

A study conducted by Kusumawati in 2010 on banking loyalty indicates that there was a decreased percentage in the number of customers still using bank services due to the dissatisfaction of the bank service delivery in Bandung city. As a result, many customers decided to move their funding to other banks. Another study by Yavas and Babakus (2008) on bank loyalty in Pakistan reinforces that it was difficult for Small and Medium Enterprises (SMEs) to be loyal to their banks because customers were still very sensitive to interest rates.

There is an indication that the change of customer behavior can be marked with how often the customers move their fund to other banks. This phenomenon of switching customer behavior often occurs with business customers. In addition, based on an interview result with individual business customers, it was found that they did not save their entire endowment in one bank alone. A further study may be suggested to examine what factors leading to customer loyalty. According to Lages et al. (2004), clients who are not well-maintained will feel uncomfortable, and in the end will leave the company. On the other hand, according to Rauyruen et al. (2007), marketers and customers will have a good quality relationship if each party is committed to maintaining their relationship.

Junarsin (2010) agrees that service products and services offered by banks were almost the same for every bank that it was so difficult to find the uniqueness. Therefore, uniqueness must be created. This may affect loyalty, whereas in the study it was revealed that some bank customers left the bank that had long been a place for their investment because it did not meet their desired expectation. However, a different study conducted by Lien-Li et al. (2012) on customer-perceived value, shows that customer-perceived value has a very low impact on loyalty. However, Yunus et al. (2009) in their study find that customer-perceived value can provide the basis for customer satisfaction and loyalty. Based on the existing phenomenon as well as the existing literature gaps, this phenomenon is worth investigating.

According to this phenomenon, the main objective of this study is to know whether bank expectation on customer loyalty can be fulfilled by the relational quality and customer-perceived value.

2 Literature Review

2.1 Customer-Perceived Value

A study by Bojei and Alwie (2010) indicates that cultural differences between western and eastern countries influence customer behaviors. Eastern countries tend prefer the high "value" by giving special treatments in maintaining long-term relationships. Moliner et al. (2006) in their research on a travel agent in Spain find that relational quality can have a positive impact on customer-perceived value. The travel agent company conducted a series of efforts so that customers remained loyal. This was conducted because many regular customers increasingly disappeared. Their findings suggest that the relational good quality can provide the customer perceived value.

2.2 Relational Quality

Rauyruen et al. (2007) in their study state that "the quality of the relationship is long-lived assets to be maintained as a competitive advantage". Kuo and Chang (2011) "relationship quality is very important in maintaining the viability of customer and corporate". Both stated that the relational quality is required in business to maintain long-term relationships as in the potential competitive advantage. They examined the relational quality applied to Business to Business companies.

Similarly, Hawkley et al. (2008) find that the relational quality is a final objective of a relationship that must be maintained by both parties so that the relationship can last long. Further in the research, the relational quality shows that the relationship occurred between two individuals indicating the closeness between the two parties.

Wu et al. (2010) suggest that customers believe in the integrity of the sales persons and entrust things to the future performance of the sales persons, based on the satisfaction consistently given by the sales persons. In the same fashion, Bojei and Alwie (2010) define that the relational quality shows customer perceptions in which the relationship is to meet the expectations, goals, and desires of customers. Relational quality is an interaction relationship with customers, and interpersonal skills are required to develop long-term relationships. The components used to measure relational quality in this study are adopted from Bojei and Alwi (2010), Jap et al. (1999) and Auruskeviciene et al. (2010) in their study, including communication effectiveness, friendliness, and trust.

2.3 Loyalty

An expert in loyalty, Oliver (1999) argues that customer loyalty is a very strong commitment to re-purchase or supports the products or services in a sustainable manner in the future, although it is influenced by the situation and marketing aspects that have the potential to switch to buy. Smets et al. (2011) state that the main focus of customer loyalty is how to keep customers so that they do not switch to other products or companies. To establish customer loyalty, companies must build good relations between the company and its products with the customers.

On the other hand, Boohene and Agyapong (2011) argue that customer loyalty is the behavior of customers trying to keep their promises on the product, buy with a higher frequency, and re-purchase by recommending to others, as well as being loyal to the brand in dealing with the company. According to Yavas and Babakus (2008), one approach to measure purchase behavior is by looking at the dimension of share of wallet. They find that the share of wallet can be justified, and can be used in measuring the marketing performance or loyalty measurement in financial institutions, such as banks.

Other researchers such as Oliver (1999), Baumman et al. (2005), like Yavas and Babakus (2008) find that Customer Loyalty is an indicator of the company's success in getting the customers. Customer loyalty consists of three dimensions, namely *Satisfaction*, the happy feeling after consuming a product or service compared to expectations, *Continued patronage*, recurrent expenditure in the same place, and *Share of Wallet*, the money being spent or invested in the bank.

Based on the problem phenomenon and literature reviews conducted, a hypothesis is made: relational quality and value perceived by customers may simultaneously increase the customer loyalty.

3 Methodology

This research was a verification study is used to reveal the relationship of the variables in this study. Verification study is a study that uses research hypotheses as the approach. Survey was conducted to collect data from the relevant population. Respondents of this study were taken from 8 banks in West Java, Indonesia, that implement e-banking with a total of 178 of business customers. Interviews and questionnaires were used to obtain data from business customers in 8 banks. Fifteen questions were asked to measure the variable of customer-perceived value, 12 questions were asked to measure relational quality, and 8 questions were asked to measure loyalty. The analysis technique used in this research is Structural Equation Modeling (SEM) based on variance structure, also known as Partial Least Square Path Modeling (PLS-PM). This research applied multistage random probability samplings, namely stratified random sampling for each bank with proportional allocation, and systematic sampling for the selection of respondents from each bank, with unlimited population.

4 Findings

In the analysis of the structural model, testing causality between the relational quality and customer-perceived value towards customer loyalty is presented below (Fig. 1).

Simultaneous Hypotheses:

H_0: $\beta_{31} = \beta_{32} = 0$ Customer Relational Quality and Customer-Perceived Value do not affect simultaneously and partially to Customer Loyalty.

H_1: $\beta_{3i} = \beta_{32} \neq 0$ Customer Relational Quality and Customer-Perceived Value affect simultaneously and partially to Customer Loyalty.

F test statistic was used to test these hypotheses with the following results:

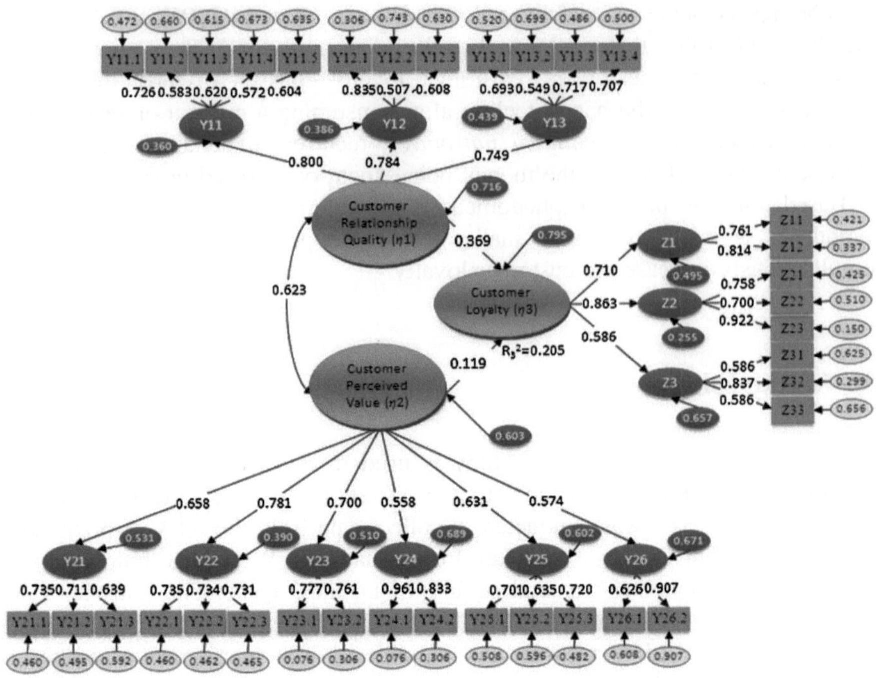

Fig. 1 The influence of customer relational quality and customer-perceived value toward customer loyalty. Description: Y11 = communication effectiveness, Y12 = friendliness, Y13 = trust, Z1 = Satisfaction, Z2 = Continued Patronage, Z3 = Share of Wallet, Y21 = Functional value of establishment, Y22 = Functional value of service purchase (profesionalism), Y23 = Functional value of service purchase (quality), Y24 = Functional value of price, Y25 = Emotional value, Y26 = Social value

Table 1 Testing of Hypothesis 1: Customer relational quality and customer-perceived value *f* do not affect simultaneously and partially to customer loyalty

Hypothesis	R^2	*F*	*F* table	Detail
H_0: $\beta_{31} = \beta_{32} = 0$ H_1: $\beta_{3i} = \beta_{32} \neq 0$	0.205	49.638	3.019	Null hypothesis is rejected

According to Table 1, changes occurred in the variable of loyalty are caused by changes occurred relational quality and customer-perceived valued simultaneously of 20.5 %. It can be concluded that null hypothesis is rejected with *F* count (49.638) bigger than the value of *F* table (3.019). This result shows that the relational quality and customer-perceived value contribute a very strong impact to customer loyalty. To find out how big is the effect of both variables partially to customer loyalty, partial testing is conducted as follows:

H_0: $\beta_{31} = 0$ Customer Relational Quality does not affect Customer Loyalty.

H_1: $\beta_{31} \neq 0$ Customer Relational Quality affects Customer Loyalty.

H_0: $\beta_{32} = 0$ Customer-Perceived Value does not affect Customer Loyalty.

Table 2 Testing of Hypothesis 2: Customer relational quality and customer-perceived value affect simultaneously and partially to customer loyalty

Effect	Effect value	R^2	*Standard error*	*T*	f^2	*t*-table	Decision
Customer relational quality → Customer loyalty	0.369	0.136	0.054	6.815	0.121	1.964	Reject null hypothesis
Customer-perceived value → Customer loyalty	0.119	0.014	0.058	2.033	0.011	1.964	Reject null hypothesis

H_1: $\beta_{32} \neq 0$ Customer-Perceived Value affects Customer Loyalty.

To test the hypotheses above, *t student* test statistic was used with the following results:

The structural equation model is as follow:

$$Customer\,Loyalty = 0.369\,relational\,quality + 0.119\,customer\,perceived\,value + \xi.$$

Table 2 shows that changes in value perceived by customers influence changes in customer loyalty by 13.6 %. Through hypothesis testing using *t student* test statistic, it shows that the customer relational quality contributes positively to loyalty. On the other hand, the value perceived towards loyalty is not strong. This is shown by the *effect size* of 0.011 that is less than 0.15. Values perceived by customers, such as perceiving the value of interest rate offered, perceiving the value of all services of Bank's employees, feeling precious to be a customer for being in an expected social level, have a small power in affecting loyalty. Customer relational quality has a bigger effect than values perceived by customers.

5 Discussion

Interestingly, finding suggests that customer relational quality has a dominant contribution to loyalty compared to customer perceived value. The reason is that customer relational quality with emotional touch maintained by employees of the bank may have caused customers to be dependent to partnership with the bank. Involving personal relationship between customers and bank employees could create comfort and trust of customers. This condition will stimulate the attachment and dependency of customers to bank employees, thus it will generate loyal customers. On the other hand, the small effect of the customer perceived value may be due to the fact that banks did not successfully conduct *value creation*, so that the added value might not be perceived by customers. With the technology advancement created by banks which provide easiness, customers can now use internet banking more than interact face to face. Thus, customers perceived value did not contribute changes to the loyal behavior of customers. This result is different from an empirical study result conducted by Yang and Peterson (2004) who state find that the customers perceived value affect the customer loyalty to financial institutions. This result is also different from a study result conducted by Roig et al. (2006) suggesting that the value perceived by bank customers strongly influences loyalty. Therefore, customer relation quality should become the bank management's attention. A good personal relationship between both parties that will lead to dependency of customers to bank should be maintained. Customers who have been greatly assisted psychologically will feel unfaithful if they put their savings into other places. Banks must be periodically monitoring changes in customer behavior because customers are dynamic, and changes in customer behavior that can lead customers to move their fund to other banks. If any change is indicated in advance, then there is a problem, and a further study on personal customers need to be conducted with a more thorough observation.

References

Auruskeviciene V, Salciuviene L, Skudiene V (2010) The relationship quality effect on customer loyalty. Pecvnia 10:23–36

Baumann C, Burton S, Elliott G (2005) Determinants of customer loyalty and share of wallet in retail banking. J Financ Serv Mark 9(3):231–248

Bojei J, Alwie A (2010) The influence of relationship quality on loyalty in service sector. Int J Econ Manag 4(1):81–100

Boohene R, Agyapong GKQ (2011) Analysis of the antecedents of customer loyalty of telecommunication industry in Ghana: The case of vodafone (Ghana). Int Bus Res 4(1):229–240

Hawkley LC, Hughes ME, Waite LJ, Masi CM, Thisted RA, Cacioppo JT (2008) From social structural factors to perceptions of relationship quality and loneliness: The Chicago health, aging, and social relations study. J Gerontol Soc Sci 63B(6):375–384

Jap SD, Manolis C, Weitz BA (1999) Relationship quality and buyer-seller interactions in channels of distribution. J Bus Res 46:303–313

Junarsin E (2010) Issues in the innovation service product process: A managerial perspective. Int J Manag 27(3) Part 2 Dec 2010

Kotler P, Keller KL (2012) Marketing management, 14th edn. Pearson, New Jersey

Kuo C, Chang C (2011) The study on the antecedents of relationship quality and loyalty of urban business club: Landmark club. J Int Manag Stud 6(2) ISSN 1993-1034

Kusumawati EW (2010) Pengaruh Manajemen Hubungan Pelanggan dan Atribut Produk terhadap Loyalitas Nasabah Mahasiswa di BNI Kantor Layanan UNPAD. Universitas Padjajaran, Bandung, Magister Manajemen

Lages C, Lages CR, Lages LF (2004) The relqual scale: A measure of relationship quality in export market ventures. J Bus Res 58:1040–1048

Leingpbul T, Thomas S, Broyles SA, Ross RH (2009) Loyalty's influences on the consumer satisfaction and (Re) purchase behavior relationship. J Consum Satis Dissatis Complain Behav 22. ABI/INFORM Global p. 36

Lien-Li, M, Green DG, Farazmand FA, Grodzki E (2012) 'Customer loyalty: Influences on three types of retail stores' shoppers', Int J Manag Mark Res 5(1)

Moliner M, Sanchez J, Rodrigues R, Callarisa L (2006). Perceived relationship quality and post purchase perceived value. An integrative framework. Eur J Mark 41(11/17):1392–1422
Oliver RL (1999) Whence customer loyalty. J Mark, p. 33
Rauyruen P, Miller KE, Barret NJ (2007) Relationship quality as a predictor of B2B customer loyalty. J Bus Res 60:21–31
Roig JCF, Garcia JS, Tena MAM, Monzonis JL (2006) Customer perceived value in banking services. Int J Bank Market 24(5):266–283
Smets J, Ergeerts G, Beyers R, Schrooyen F, Ceulemans M, Wante L, Renckens K (2011) An NFC-based customer loyalty system. In: The first international conference on mobile services, resources, and user. ISBN: 978-1-61208-164-9
Wu JM, Yang D, Huang J (2010) The research development and prospects of relationship quality in relationship marketing, pp 1–9
Yang Z, Peterson R (2004) Customer perceived value, satisfaction and loyalty: the rolls of switching costs. Psychol Market 21(10):799–822
Yavas U, Babakus E (2008) Retail store loyalty: a comparison of two customer segments. Int J Retail Distrib Manag 37(6):477–492
Yunus NKY, Ismail A, Juga ZR, Ishak S (2009) Service quality dimensions, perceive value and customer satisfaction: ABC relationship model testing. IBEJ 2(1):1–18

Improving Business Performance Through Entrepreneur Motivation and Value Creation on Small and Medium Enterprises

Yuyus Suryana, Iwan Mulyawan and Rita Komaladewi

Abstract The main goal of government program for Small and Medium Enterprises (SMEs) is to support SMEs in enhancing their performance, since SMEs' performance has not meet government's expectation. Several indicators showed that SMEs still have low competitive advantage, high mortality rate, and slow pace of change from small to medium enterprises and medium to big enterprises. The main objective of this research was to study how entrepreneurship motivation affects value creation and performance of SMEs. The descriptive and explanatory methods were applied. Data was obtained from SMEs of West Java Province, Indonesia, which has survived in their business for at least three years. This study utilized cross sectional time horizon to obtain current situation of the objects. The hypotheses of this research were tested using statistic methods of Structural Equation Modeling (SEM) with 217 samples. The results of this study showed that entrepreneurship motivation positively affected value creation and value creation affected business performance. Also, entrepreneurship motivation became a driver to conduct innovation creation. It was also found that, generally, the performance of SMEs strongly depended on the success of implementing value creation as a business strategy.

Keywords Entrepreneurship motivation · Value creation · Business performance · Small and medium enterprise

Y. Suryana (✉) · R. Komaladewi
Department of Management and Business, Universitas Padjadjaran, Bandung, Indonesia
e-mail: yuyus.suryana@yahoo.com
URL: http://www.fe.unpad.ac.id

R. Komaladewi
e-mail: rita.komaladewi@fe.unpad.ac.id
URL: http://www.fe.unpad.ac.id

I. Mulyawan
Politeknik Negeri Bandung, Bandung, Indonesia
e-mail: imulyawan56@yahoo.com
URL: http://www.polban.ac.id

S. Soh (ed.), *Selected Papers from the Asia Conference on Economics & Business Research 2015*, DOI 10.1007/978-981-10-0986-0_3

1 Introduction

The economy in the third millennium is now including not only international but also global economy, where traffic circulation of goods and services commodity is massive and fast, supported by ICT (*Information Communication Technology*) and rapid, reliable transportation system; so it is true what Thomas Friedman (2006) suggests that "the world is flat" and eventually becomes a "global Village." A country can be said to participate in international trade if it has an indicator showing an increase in the rate of export and import reflected from the increase of export share in global market and the increase of import ratio to its gross domestic product (GDP). The more active the process of production that involves many countries, the greater flow the foreign investment into the country, or the greater investment from the country to other countries.

Furthermore, Forsman and Temel (2011) argue that SMEs are the engine of economic growth, and innovation as a form of value creation is a tool for SMEs to improve competitiveness, as well as improving business performance.

Alam et al. (2013) conducted a research on SMEs and suggested that there is a connection between innovation and competitiveness, and the performance improvement proposed. On the other hand, Heunks (1998) argues that innovation also improves financial performance, as the success indicator for SMEs.

As explained by Kasali (2010), economy that relies on conglomerate business was proven to be unable to overcome multi-dimensional crisis, including economy, which also caused unemployment. On the other hand, small and medium enterprises including micro enterprises were proven to be reliable. They also were considered as resilient, independent, flexible in mobility, efficient, does not rely on debt, and are based on local resources. SME doers are mostly both the owners and managers, and they are innovative, willing to take risk, and proactive businessmen (Wiklund and Shepherd 2005).

Related to West Java, according to the Department of Cooperation, micro, small, and medium Enterprises of the Province of West Java (2011), there are 8,731,790 business units of micro, small, and medium enterprises (MSMEs), whereas the number of micro enterprises is 8,616,254 units, small enterprises of 10,692 units, medium enterprises of 7408 units, and large enterprises of 1536 business units. According to the result of a specifically conducted survey in 2012, the most dominant constraint for SMEs is the inability to compete and capital.

Mortality problem that occurred in small and medium enterprises (SMEs) is not only a problem for Indonesia, but also for other countries. It is stated that the ups and downs of SMEs depend on the business motivation, including the characteristics and persistency of SME doers individually. There were well-developed SMEs, but there are also SMEs that went bankrupt, only 50 % of SMEs left that still survive and develop after they are 10 years old. In addition, Chupp (2010) from Toledo University of Canada also argued that for the past decades, SMEs have contributed to economic growth by 70 %, the creation of employment by 70 %,

99.5 % of employers work in this sector (SMEs), but more than 60 % of them failed in 6 years of period. This was due to the inability to compete.

Based on the explanation of the research background, this topic is worth studying because the role of small and medium enterprises is very important and strategic, particularly in the national economy and in the level of the province of West Java, because of their role in overcoming unemployment.

It can be pointed that motivation of entrepreneurs is one of the causes of the declining ability to compete as well as the ability of entrepreneurs in creating value. Value creation can be seen by emphasizing the innovation aspect, not only the product, process, or organization (as an independent variable), but also its implication for business performance.

The unit analysis of this research is small businesses in the Province of West Java, focusing on processing or manufacture and trade industries considering that this is the most reliable sector with the most population in business area, both nationally and in West Java. Therefore, the objectives of this research are (1) Does entrepreneurial motivation affect positively the value creation of the company's innovation? (2) Does innovation value creation affect positively the business performance? (3) Does entrepreneurial motivation affect the innovation value creation that implicates business performance?

Based on the explanation given above, the objective of this research is to create a model which has the ability to explain the problems in SMEs performance in the Province of West Java and to predict the variables tested.

2 Literature Review

2.1 Entrepreneurial Motivation

Entrepreneurial motivation is important because failure is an integral part or attached to business behavior, particularly in the process of becoming a successful entrepreneurship. Bessant and dan Tidd (2011) argues that an entrepreneur may fail but not the person, because an entrepreneur will learn from the failure or the failure will become a part in the process toward success. Next, Bessant and Tidd (2011) propose that entrepreneurship will be a driving force to innovate in creating value for customers, businesses, and socials. In addition, Kemelgor and Bruce (2002), Wiklund and Shepherd (2005) state that there is a positive and significant relation between entrepreneurship orientation (**innovation**, risk taker, and proactive) to business performance. On the other hand, Smith, Guthrie, and Chen (1989) state that business performance is not influenced by entrepreneurship orientation. Then, Wiklund (1999) state that several studies have shown that entrepreneurship orientation affects innovation in long term, not in the short term. Shane et al. (2003) argues that the will to achieve high performance in business is an important motivation to be a reliable entrepreneur.

2.2 Value Innovation

Furthermore, Bessant and Tidd (2011) argue that entrepreneurship will be a driving force to innovate creating value for customers, businesses, and socials. This is confirmed by Bessant and Tidd (2011) that creating value is the meaning and purpose of an innovation that is expressed in financial, growth, employment, business continuity, or the increase of social welfare. Gunday et al. (2009) states that innovation is an instrument of growth strategy in entering new market, which is used to increase market share and to make the company more competitive. In globalization context, innovation business is a component in corporation strategies.

2.3 Business Performance

A study by Covin (1991) measured business performance of its financial performance with a 5-point Likert scale. Financial performance can be seen from sales level, sales growth rate, cash flow, ROE, gross profit margin, net profit from operation, profit to sales ratio, ROI, and the ability to fund business growth from profit. This study employs the measurement of ability to generate profits or how far business can be managed effectively and efficiently. These measurements do not question the business scale. Hughes (2002) concludes that the success of innovation and its impact to business performance will last depending on managerial skills and competence of the company. Gunday et al. (2009) confirms that the effect of innovation to business performance has a positive correlation. The innovation includes product, process, and organizational innovations. According to the research plan, hypotheses can be drawn.

Hypothesis 1
Entrepreneurial motivation affects innovation value creation of small and medium enterprises in the Province of West Java.

Hypothesis 2
Innovation value creation affects business performance of small and medium enterprises in the Province of West Java.

3 Methodologies

This was a causality research, testing the cause–effect relationship between independent and dependent variables. Analysis unit of this research was organizations, the small and medium enterprises in the Province of West Java, with the doers particularly the leaders of SMEs in manufacture and trade industries as the unit of observation. This was a cross sectional research, where survey was conducted in a period of time. Samples were taken from companies that had been running ≥3 years, where they had survived with all entrepreneurship motivations and orientations. Samples were taken randomly and 217 samples were used. Structural Equation Modeling (SEM) was used as statistic method for analysis.

4 Finding

To test the hypotheses, statistic of the student test was used with the test result as shown in Table 1.

Based on the test result, it can be seen that the value of t_{count} of entrepreneurial motivation variable (9.850) is bigger than $t_{critical}$ (1.96). Therefore, based on the rest result, it can be concluded that entrepreneurial motivation affects the value creation or innovation of the small medium enterprises in West Java positively (Table 2).

There is an effect of entrepreneurial motivation to value creation with a coefficient of determination R^2 of 73.7 % in SMEs in West Java Province, while the remaining 26.3 % is the effect of other factors not examined by this study. On the other hand, the effect of innovation value creation to business performance is 65.5 % in SMEs, while the remaining 34.5 % is the effect of other factors not examined in this study. High innovation value creation of SME doers will increase business performance of small and business enterprises in West Java (Table 3).

Table 1 The test result of the effect of entrepreneurial motivation to innovation value creation

Path coef.	T_{count}	$T_{critical}$	Ho	Ha
0.859	9.850	1.96	Rejected	Accepted

Table 2 Structural model

Sub structure	Path	Coefficient	T^{a}_{count}	R-Square
First	EM → VC	0.859	9.850	0.737
Second	VC → BP	0.809	10.315	0.655

[a] $t_{critical} = 1.96$

Source Processed data, output result of AMOS 20

Table 3 Test result of the effect of innovation value creation to business performance

Path Coef.	T_{count}	$T_{critical}$	Ho	Ha
0.809	10.315	1.96	Rejected	Accepted

[*] $t_{critical} = 1.96$

Source Processed data, output result of AMOS 20

Based on the test result, it can be seen that the value of t_{count} of entrepreneurial motivation variable (10.315) is bigger than $t_{critical}$ (1.96). Thus, based on the test result, it can be concluded that value creation affect business performance of small and medium enterprises in West Java positively.

This condition strengthens the previous study by Forsman and Temel (2011), Tidd and Bessant (2011) that the aspect of innovation affects business performance significantly. This becomes clear because innovation will increase competitive advantage, both directly and indirectly, for companies as well as create value for consumers (Cravens and Piercy 2013) (Fig. 1).

Government's program is the most dominant in supporting entrepreneurial motivation is the availability for both good infrastructure and access to model in developing business. The marketing strategy by Igor Ansoff Matrix (Kotler 2006)

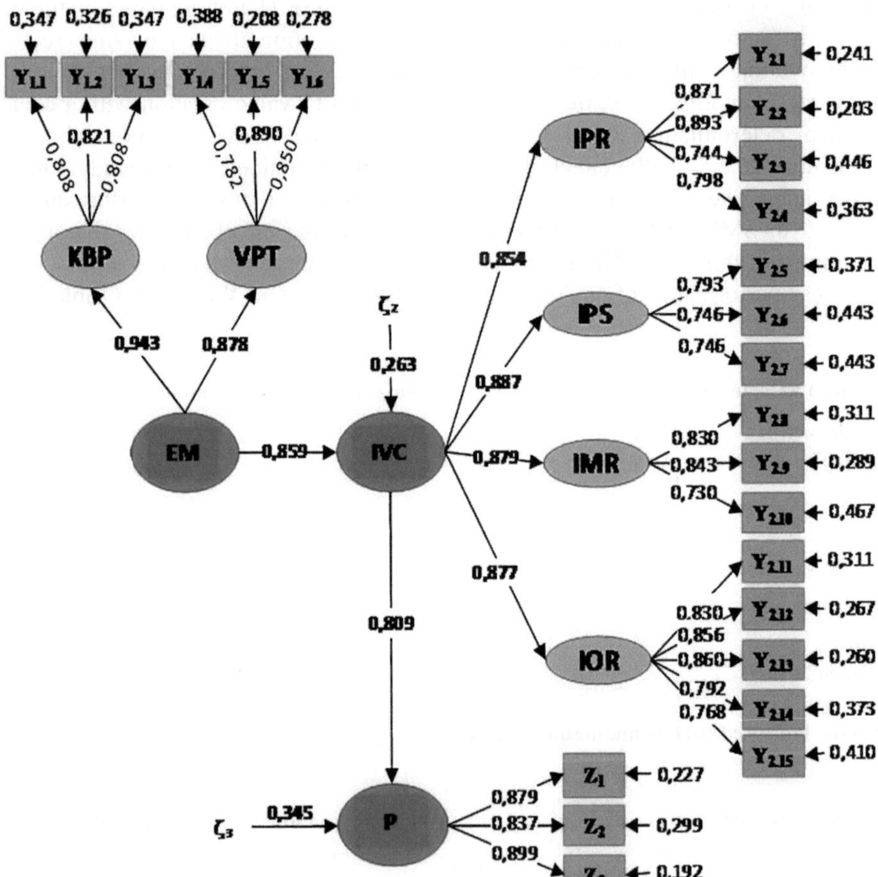

Fig. 1 Model structure of the influence of entrepreneur motivation toward innovation value creation and impact to performance

can be used in this matter, namely marketing penetration strategy where existing products are allocated for the market at a price lower the average prices of competitors on the assumption that SMEs are innovation in the process with an emphasis on efficiency. Companies carry out innovation-based product development both incremental and radical innovation. In addition, SMEs can also implement the concept of marketing strategy by Michael Porter (Craven and Piercy 2013), namely the innovation of process aimed at building low cost so that the output price is cheaper, or by attempting to create differentiated product whose difference is considered important by the consumer. Finally, in marketing the products, SMEs have to focus on their targeted markets, and market segmentation is needed in the process so that the marketing effort become more focused.

5 Discussion

From the hypotheses, it is revealed that entrepreneurial motivation and value creation of motivation are dominant factors in increasing business performance. Based on the formulation of the problems, the factors needed to be considered to enhance business performance, including Government's Program (forming factors of entrepreneurial motivation), are infrastructure, education and training, and marketing and R&D aspects for internal empowerment. Next, innovation value creation is the product that uses alternative and innovative materials, innovation in delivery process, innovation in promotion and pricing technique, and everything should be within the framework of innovation organizationally so that all can be facilitated well structurally, in management of procedural innovation and information system.

For Research and Development or R&D, although it only has produced the incremental products and not the radical one, this department is important and strategic in sustaining business continuity, particularly in sustaining competitive advantage. This is impossible because innovation value creation will only grow and be developed by R&D's effort.

Entrepreneurial motivation also becomes a driven force for the creation of innovation.

Regarding the variable innovation creation value, it can be seen from the verification research that generally the high performance of SMEs strongly depend on the success of running the innovation value creation as a business strategy. The creation of innovation value includes product, process, marketing, and organizational elements. The effectiveness of innovation value creation will be realized if organizational innovation is built first so that the creation of product, process, and marketing innovation can run effectively, considering that organizational aspect is the platform for the effectiveness of company program implementation.

To develop innovative products and processes for SMEs, the cooperation between universities in West Java should be improved, considering they have been doing a lot of applied researches, which can be developed into prototypes of product for marketing test, in addition to carrying community service. On the other hand, collaboration researches or joint researches can be conducted in order to reach a mutually beneficial cooperation.

SMEs also need to develop business on the basis of innovation value creation because it is very important and strategic to build competitiveness and achieve superior business performance. Therefore, in business management, HRD, marketing, financial, and production should be developed. Business management is important, particularly in the aspect of how to develop a competitive business through product, production process, marketing, and organizational innovations.

References

Alam S, Varan V, Nor M, Kahappan, Fang LS (2013) Relationship between innovation capabilities, business performance, marketing performance. Bus and Manag Horiz

Bessant J, dan Tidd J (2011) Innovation and entrepreneurship, 2nd edn. Wiley, Hoboken

Cravens DW and Nigel FP (2013) Strategic marketing, 10th edn. New York:Mc Graw-Hill

Covin J, Green K and Slevin D (2006) Strategic process on the entrepreneurial orientation-sales growth relationship. Entrepreneurship Theory and Practice. 30(1):57–82

Chupp BK (2010) An analysis of the learning processes of successful entrepreneurs, University of Toledo

Dess GG, Lumpkin GT, Covin JG (1997) Entrepreneurial strategy making and firm performance: test contingency and configurational models. Strateg Manage J 18(9):677–695

Forsman H and Temel S (2011) Innovation and business performance in small enterprises: an enterprise-level analysis. Int J Innov Manag 15(3):641–665

Gunday G, Ulusoy G, Kilic K, Alpkan L (2009) Effects of innovation types of firm performance. Gebze Institute of Technology, Department of Management, No:101, 41400, Cayirova Gebze-Kocaeli, Turkey

Heunks FJ (1998) Innovation, creativity and success. Small Bus Econ 10(3):263–272

Hughes A (2002) Innovation and business performance small enterprises: firms in the UK and the EU. Institute of Management Studies Centre for Business Research University Cambridge

Kasali R (2010) Modul Kewirausahaanuntuk program Strata 1. HikmahZamanBaru, Jakarta

Kemelgor and Bruce H (2002) A comparative analysis of corporate entrepreneurial orientation between selected firms: in the Netherlands and the USA. Entrepreneurship Reg Dev 14(1): 67–87

Kotler PDK (2006) Marketing Management. 12th edn. Prentice Hall International Inc. A division of Simon & Schuster, Englewood Cliffs, NJ07632

Kyrgidou LP, Hughes M (2010) Strategic entrepreneurship: origins, core elements and research directions. Eur Bus Rev 22(1)

Scarborough NM, Zimmerer T (2003) Effective small business management: an entrepreneurial approach. Prentice Hall

Shane S, Venkataraman S (2000) The promise of entrepreneurship as a field of research. Acad Manage Rev 25:217–226

Shane SA (2008) The illusions of entrepreneurship: the costly myths that entrepreneurs, investors, and policy makers live by. Yale University Press, New Haven

Smith KG, Guthrie JP, Chen MJ (1989) Strategy, size and performance prganization studies, 10(1)

Wiklund J, Shepherd D (2005) Entrepreneurial orientation and small business performance: a configurational approach. J Bus Ventur 20:71–91

Analysis of Expectation Disconfirmation, Students Satisfaction, and University Image Toward E-WoM Intention Through Social Media: A Case Study of an Entrepreneurial University in Jakarta

Puji Rahayuningtyas and Liza Agustina Maureen Nelloh

Abstract Since the number of entrepreneurs is still 1.65 % from the total population in Indonesia, several universities in Jakarta begins to boost entrepreneurial spirit to young people through implementing entrepreneurial-based university. The research contributes to service recovery and improvement of marketing strategy to grab upcoming students. Thus, this research aims to analyze expectation disconfirmation (EDT), students' satisfaction and University image toward WoM intention on social media in an entrepreneurial university in Jakarta. To answer research aims, the researchers use Structural Equation Model (SEM) analysis with Partial Least Square (PLS) technique. The questionnaires were distributed to 121 students who have joined the university at least for a year by using purposive sampling technique. The result of this research indicates that all variables tested are related to each other, yet the lowest loading factor was on EDT. Thus, the entrepreneurial university should improve the promotional strategy to avoid over promising.

Keywords Expectation disconfirmation (EDT) · Students' satisfaction · University image · E-WoM · Entrepreneurial university

1 Introduction

Litbang Kompas/12032015/h.18/RH on Marketing Research Indonesia, stated that total entrepreneurs in Indonesia is still 1.65 % from 25,361 million total population in Indonesia. To compare, Japan has 10 %, Singapore 7 %, Malaysia 5 %, and

P. Rahayuningtyas (✉) · L.A.M. Nelloh
Entrepreneurship Study Program, Podomoro University, Jakarta, Indonesia
e-mail: puji.rahayuningtyas@podomorouniversity.ac.id

L.A.M. Nelloh
e-mail: liza.nelloh@podomorouniversity.ac.id

S. Soh (ed.), *Selected Papers from the Asia Conference on Economics & Business Research 2015*, DOI 10.1007/978-981-10-0986-0_4

Thailand 3 % in the same period. This means that Indonesia needs big effort to boost the number of entrepreneurs because it is believed that economics are quite dependent on entrepreneurial spirit. Whereas, in the result of the Global Entrepreneurship Monitor survey in 2013, it is revealed that Indonesia holds second rank in the willingness to become an entrepreneur.

One of the factors why Indonesia has a lack of entrepreneurs, especially young entrepreneurs, is that there is no entrepreneurial character building since young age; they tend to be trained to work rather than create a job field. To support, Witjaksono, Finance Director of PT. Dwi Aneka Jaya Kemasindo stated that "*Kebanyakan para orang tua selalu menanamkan dan mempersiapkan anak mereka menjadi pekerja ketimbang menjadi pengusaha,*" (Most of parents train their child to be an employee instead of hiring employees). This mindset becomes a concern for some academics.

Hence, the government takes a responsibility to change the mindset of the society. It is proved by a regulatory in curriculum 2013 that entrepreneurship must be taught in senior high school. Viewing this phenomenon, universities as the highest level of formal education take a chance also. Some universities in Jakarta are competing in creating entrepreneurial-based programs to produce young entrepreneurs and to educate them with the soul of entrepreneurship with all facilities offered.

Since the students are living in the high-tech era and are very critical, they tend to easily share their experience to the world through Internet. The Internet has changed the way customers communicate by providing a common space to share opinions and reviews (Goldsmith and Horowitz 2006) and their opinions are freely read by others around the world, thus, have hug potential reach (Hennig-Thurau and Walsh 2004). This kind of communication process is known as electronic word-of-mouth (E-WoM). Therefore, treatment for them in facilities or service is the key to their satisfaction; fulfill their expectation through positive performances as it is strongly related to building an image of university. Since customers can easily post visual information (e.g., pictures, videos) to convey product information and consumption-related experience powered by email, blogs, interest, experiences, these E-WoM are seen as more credible, because customers tend to trust interpersonal sources rather than non-personal or commercial sources. Customers often rely on informal E-WoM when they seek information. As a result, generating positive E-WoM becomes crucial technique to build and maintain strong brand relationship with highly engaged customers (Smith et al. 2007).

2 Literature Review

2.1 Expectation Disconfirmation Theory (EDT)

EDT has long been a dominant marketing paradigm for studying customer satisfaction across many products and services (Tse and Wilton 1998). In an EDT literature

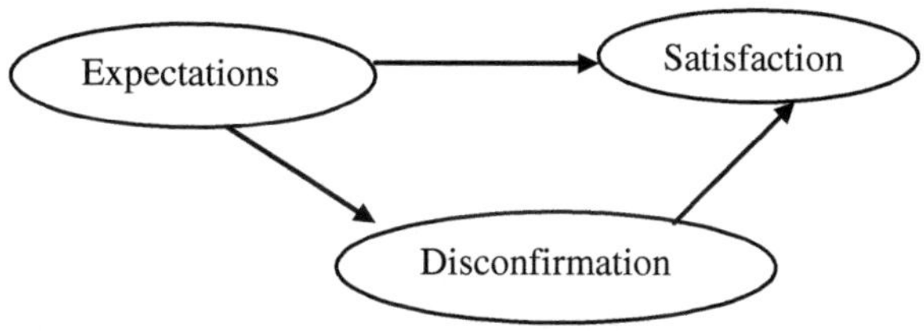

Fig. 1 The simplified expectation disconfirmation (Oliver 1977)

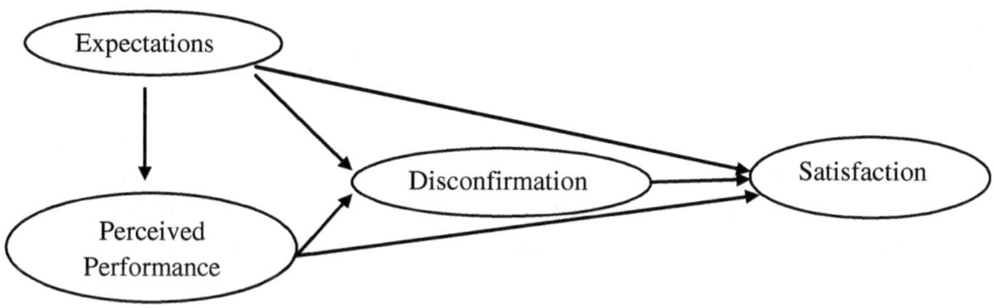

Fig. 2 The complete expectation disconfirmation model (Oliver 1977)

overview, Oliver (1977) divides into two, they are: (1) simplified expectation disconfirmation model (hereafter called as simplified model) which includes expectation, disconfirmation and satisfaction (Fig. 1); (2) complete expectation disconfirmation model. This model contains performance as an additional variable (Fig. 2).

Simplified expectation disconfirmation model describes that expectation is potential to create negative influence in disconfirmation and satisfaction. Higher expectation is more likely to be negatively disconfirmed. It usually happened when reality is lower than expectations.

Performance as an additional variable on complete expectation disconfirmation model shows that expectations tend to give positive influence on performance. The difference between simplified and complete is the inclusion of performance and its relationship with the other EDT variables. Furthermore, in the complete disconfirmation model performance is positively related to disconfirmation, how performance is converted into psychological (disconfirmation) (Oliver 1989). It is said that the higher the performance, the more likely performance will exceed expectations, resulting in positive disconfirmation. Trust grows when trust is positively confirmed or declined, but is destroyed or declined when trust is negatively disconfirmed (Lewicki and Buncker 1996).

EDT itself can measure customers' satisfaction from the difference between customers' expectation and customers' experience in perceived products and services in multiple manners of customers. Figure 2 consists of four components:

expectations, perceived performance, disconfirmation, and satisfaction which are discussed as follow:

Expectations define the customer's anticipations about performance of product and services (Churchill and Surprenant 1982). Since EDT is capable of defining multiple manners of customers, there is an initial expectation of customers that use specific product or service is based on previous experience and also an initial expectation of customers that belong to new customers, they have no specific previous experience of quality or performance of products or service they tend to purchase. These two kind of initial expectations create a difference. The initial expectation of such new customers consists of feedbacks that they receive from other customers, advertisement, and mass media. On the other hand, another initial expectation of customers who have previous experience is close to reality. Therefore, they do repurchasing (Haistead and Hartman 1994).

Perceived performance investigates the customers' experience after using products or services that can be better or worse than customers' expectation (Spreng and MacKenzie 1996). Both types of customers who have previous experience and who do not have such experience will use purchased products or service for a while and realize its actual quality.

Disconfirmation is defined as the difference between custmers' initial expectation and observed actual performance (Bhattacherjee and Premkumar 2004). According to literature, disconfirmation is divided into three types. They are: positive disconfirmation, negative disconfirmation, and simple disconfirmation. It is said as a negative disconfirmation when actual performance of the product or service cannot meet customers' expectation, and it will lead to customers' dissatisfaction. On the other hand, positive disconfirmation will occur if perceived performance of certain product or service meet or even exceed customers' satisfaction. In the end, if there is no difference between customer's expectation and actual performance then the perceived performance equals the expectation; as a result, simple disconfirmation occurs (Oliver 1989; Santos and Boote 2003).

According to McKnight (2005), EDT is measured through several dimensions such as, functionality, reliability, helpfulness, usefulness, and easy to use. However, the term of service would not be suitable for the easy to use which is suitable for intangible product (McKnight 2005). Functionality is defined as the degree to which the technology will have the capability, functions, or features needed to accomplish one's task(s). Therefore, reliability is defined as the degree to which the technology will continually operate properly, or will operate in a consistent and flawless manner. McKnight (2005) defined helpfulness as the degree to which technology will provide adequate and responsive help, and users with helpfulness trusting expectation will anticipate that a system has an adequate help function. Helpfulness bears a slight similarity to benevolence trusting beliefs in interpersonal trust relationships in which the trustee cares about one's needs and acts in one's best interest. Thus, places usefulness as a characteristic of automation trust, as individuals can rely on or trust that a useful system is beneficial (Sheridan 1988).

2.2 Students' Satisfaction

Customer satisfaction has been defined by Rust and Oliver (1994) as the "customer's fulfillment response," which is an assessment and an emotion-based reaction to a service provided. Nicolescu (2005) believed that students are the customers of the university and survival. In short, student satisfaction will be the important term for the university to survive. Many researchers defined how important customer satisfaction is. Regarding EDT concept, if customers realize that perceived information of product or service can satisfy their initial expectations, then the occured positive disconfirmation leads to the satisfaction. Yet, if the perceived information they obtained does not match with their initial satisfaction, then negative disconfirmation leads to customer's dissatisfaction.

Expectations itself are defined as a set of standards that predict expectations and perceptions of customers about specific product or service (Bearden and Teel 1993). Figure 3 below shows on how expectations affects perceived performance in EDT model. According to Fig. 3, expectations have positive impact on perceived performance and make positive relationship toward disconfirmation. Then, disconfirmation generates positive effects on overall satisfaction that consist of both positive and negative disconfirmation (Yi 1990). To conclude, this figure proves that performance has direct impact on overall satisfaction. Overall satisfaction is understood as customer's satisfaction of previous purchase experience from websites that such a satisfaction can include all different aspects, like: customer's information satisfaction, online facilities satisfaction, and purchase satisfaction.

To summarize, EDT has two crucial variables that are expectation and experience or perceived performance. These two variables function to divide the time periods. Expectation is related to pre-purchase time period that a customer has an initial expectation toward specific or certain performance, such as quality of product or service. Experience or perceived performance is related to after purchase time

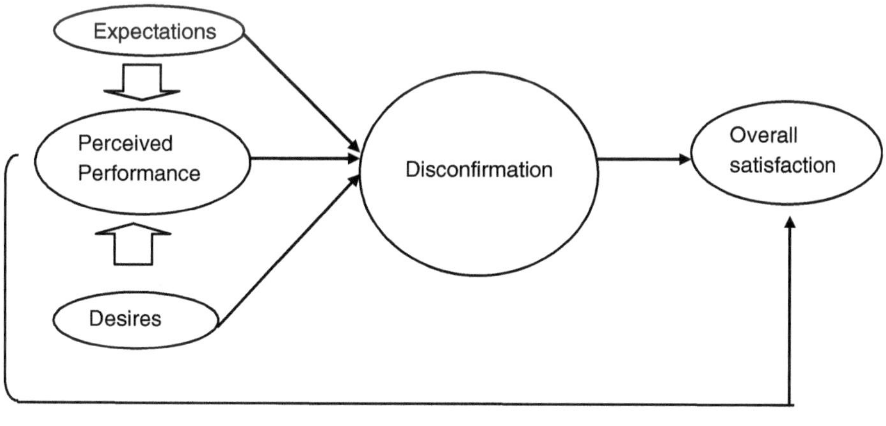

Fig. 3 Expectations and disconfirmation model

period that the customer gets experience after perceiving a real performance of the product or services. To highlight, the underlying difference between initial expectation and perceived experience or performance is termed as disconfirmation of expectation (Bhattacherjee and Premkumar 2004).

Again, when customer's perceived performance about the quality of products or services are higher than customer's satisfaction, will lead to positive disconfirmation. In the same way, when the customers perceived the performance worse than what they expected, negative disconfirmation occured. Based on Yi (1990), positive disconfirmation leads to customer satisfaction and negative disconfirmation will not lead to customer's satisfaction. Santos and Boote (2003) explains that positive disconfirmation and customer's behavior along satisfaction or dissatisfaction transparently.

A conceptual framework that consists of expectations, customer's satisfaction, or dissatisfaction and customer's behavior is clearly discussed by Santos and Boote (2003). The relationship is illustrated on Fig. 4. It is obviously seen that different kinds of expectations lead to customers' satisfaction and failure in meeting that different kinds of expectations causes dissatisfaction feeling in customers that results to customer's behavior.

On Fig. 4, it is explained that customers' expectations have different levels consisting two zones: intolerable and tolerable. In tolerable zone, the small difference between customer's expectations and perceived performance will create

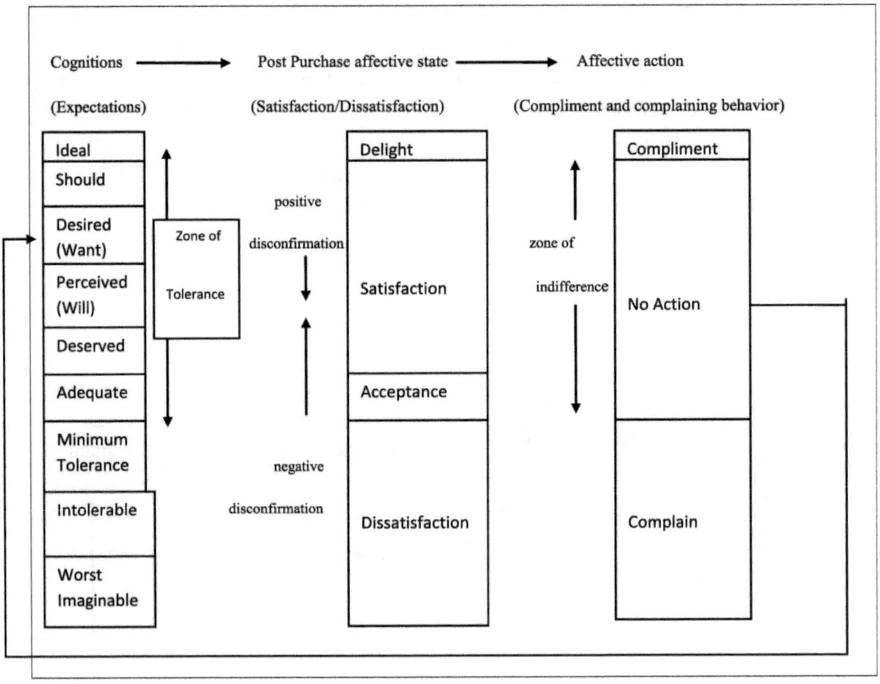

Fig. 4 Conceptual framework of EDT

dissatisfaction which is shown in part 2, while three variables stated in tolerable zone are predictable. First, when perceived performance is adequate and acceptable compared to customer's expectation will create an acceptable result but negative disconfirmation. It is caused by the inability to produce higher level of satisfaction for customers. Second, when perceived performance is getting very close to desired will create satisfaction or delight feeling of customers, and disconfirmation of this will be positive as its performance makes high level of satisfaction. Last but not least, on third part indicates customer's behavior which is based on perceived satisfaction or dissatisfaction. High satisfaction or even delight feeling of customers will lead to compliment behavior and as it is seen, dissatisfied customers lead to complain behavior. According to the explanation earlier, the researchers proposed the first hypothesis as follows:

Hypothesis 1: The Expectation Disconfirmation has a positive effect on students' satisfaction.

Therefore, there are lots of studies which conclude that customer satisfaction is initiated by brand image or corporate image. However, Helm et al. (2007) focus on balance theory. Balance theory states that individuals strive for consistency in their knowledge system, their perceptions of themselves and their environment and they try to avoid any inconsistencies in this regard. In more detail, Heider conceptualizes social relations as a triad, consisting of two individuals and one impersonal entity both individuals are related to such as an idea or an object. Whether a structure is balanced or not depends on the combination of positive and negative relations among the triad's constituents. Thus, it is concluded that if a consumer makes a positive experience with a company's product, she is supposed to perceive a feeling of satisfaction. If then she is asked to indicate the reputation of the company that made a product (a company otherwise hardly known to the individual) she is very likely to rank it highly. Ascribing the company a bad image or reputation would create a state of imbalance and therefore cause cognitive dissonance. In order to avoid this disequilibrium and maintain/reestablish cognitive consonance, the consumer will be likely to adapt her opinion about the company's reputation to the already existing level of satisfaction (Helm et al. 2007). Hence, it could be applied also on higher education sector. If students have a positive experience with the university or they felt satisfied with the university then simultaneously they felt the university has a good reputation. Based on those explanations the second hypothesis proposed as follows:

Hypothesis 2: Students satisfaction has a positive effect on university image.

University Image

University image derived from the famous term of image. Based on Sevier (1994), an image is a set of attitudes or beliefs that a person or audience holds about an institution. An image is how you look, and an image is who you are (Sevier 1994). Image is a notion which an individual holds with regards to another individual, group or organization. In other words, image is an impression which an individual or a group seeks to create or strike upon others regarding himself/herself/itself. On the basis of these explanations, corporate image, shortly, can be explained as all kinds of impressions that the community makes about a corporation. Corporate image is a valuable, tangible entity which is hard to imitate and it can help to obtain superior, sustainable financial performance (Marteson 2007). Kazoleas et al. (2001) proposed image as the organizational, personal, and environmental factors in the processing of the public's perception on the university image shows that receiver-oriented and audiencE-specific corporate image may vary. Brown and Dacin (1997) claim university's image derives from customers' perceptions of capability and social responsibility. Hence, it is concluded that university image is perceptual conception in the mind of customer such as students itself.

Word-of-mouth is a highly desirable sponsorship outcome, since it is widely recognized today as one of the most effective communication tools (Jiewanto et al. 2012). Thus, Jiewanto et al. (2012) concluded that a positive image can influence the intention of student to spread the word-of-mouth. Institutions can build positive emotional attachment such as university image toward the students and the students will spread a positive electronic word-of-mouth which is famous in today's business. Therefore, based on those explanations, the researchers proposed the hypothesis as follows:

Hypothesis 3: University image has a positive effect on electronic word-of-mouth intention.

Electronic Word-of-Mouth Intention (E-WoM)

Word-of-mouth intention correlated with behavioral intention as proposed by Naik et al. (2010). Word-of-mouth has been frequently addressed in the business literature especially in service literature. Classically, it has been viewed as an element in the framework that constructed from satisfaction-profit relationship (Ghorban and Tahernejad 2012). According to Mikalef et al. (2013) stated that electronic word-of-mouth intention is the sharing of information that a consumer will proceed to after he has engaged in the shopping process.

Mikalef also concluded that E-WoM as it is referral marketing is also termed is an aspect that is cited by practitioners and scholars at an increasing rate. This fact is attributed the importance which it is gaining, since more empirical studies reveal that positive word-of-mouth has an impact on new consumers attraction. Therefore, users tend to share information on a product that they have seen and would be of interest to friends and peers, a typical action of post-browsing. Being familiar with a product and aware of recent product trends also leads to relatively high levels of word-of-mouth activity (Mikalef et al. 2013).

Generally, WoM has been found to provide an easy, credible source of information and more effective than ads since customers cannot know anything and so should turn to others for information even recommendation. Customers may fall on negative word-of-mouth if service failure occured. Participating in negative word-of-mouth or complaining behavior is lessened by a company's reaction to complaint. In addition, a company's reaction to complaints influences the degree to which customers participate in negative WoM.

Comparing traditional WoM, electronic WoM (E-WoM), especially on social media is more useful due to its speed, convenience, onE-to-many reach, and its absence of facE-to-face pressure (Phelps et al. 2004). Traditional WoM communication consists of spoken words exchange with someone else in a facE-to-face situation, while E-WoM involve transmitting personal experiences and opinions through the written word (Bickart and Schindler 2001). Chu (2009) has found that customer's satisfaction with purchasing experiences has effect on customer's commitment and positive word-of-mouth intentions.

The advance of technologies has enabled customers to share product-related information via Internet, thereby increasing the impact of WoM, E-WoM itself is defined as "*any positive or negative statement made by potential, actual or former customers about a product or a company, which is made available to a multitude of people and institutions* via *the Internet*" (Hennig-Thurau and Walsh 2004, p. 60). Because of this, customers are really borderless and can share opinions through different platforms which facilitate the creation and exchange of user-generated content or usually referred as social media (Kaplan and Haenlein 2010). Social media includes Web channels, such as blogs, social network sites and forums, and it is claimed that E-WoM communications are more persistence and accessible (Hennig-Thurau and Walsh 2004). Besides, E-WoM communications are more measurable and observable comparing to traditional WoM communications (Lee et al. 2008).

3 Methodology

A total of 19 observed variables constitute the measurement of exogenous and endogenous variables. The independent variable of expectation disconfirmation consist of seven items, university image as a mediating variable consist of four items, hence students' satisfaction consist of four items. E-WoM intention as dependent variable in this study consisting four items scale. The scaling applied in this study is the 5-point Likert scale of 5-strongly agree, 4-agree, 3-neutral, 4-strongly disagree, and 1-strongly disagree.

A purposive technique of sample distribution was applied in this study. The authors also convinced that each of the questionnaires from previous studies literatures. It was distributed to 163 students and it returned for 121 questionnaires which contained 74.23 % in response rate. Furthermore, this study used Structural

Equation Model (SEM) and Partial Least Square (PLS) method of its robustness against distributional constraints as compared to covariancE-based analysis methods (Chin 1998). Thus, PLS also a useful tool for estimating the measurement model of latent constructs by means of linear combinations of their empirical indicators and the structural models between constructs, then, PLS has flexible assumptions for a sample distribution, the smaller sample size required for model estimation is the crucial advantage of PLS when only a relatively small sample size is available (Chin et al. 2003).

4 Results and Discussion

The respondents' profile in this study would be kindly seen in Table 1. Table 1 represented the gender, major, and one descriptive question "Does the university enjoyable for you?"

4.1 Respondents' Profile

The table reports the respondents in this study are more on females (55 %) than males (45 %). The respondents are dominated from Entrepreneurship Department (28 %) and Hotel Business Program (26 %). Thus, this study confirmed the entrepreneurial university would be entitled as enjoyable campus which is 85 % of students felt happy to study there.

Table 1 Respondents' profile

Characteristics	Total	Percentage (%)
		Sample = 121
Gender		
Male	54	45
Female	67	55
Major		
Entrepreneurship	34	28
Hotel business program	31	26
Construction engineering and management	25	21
Architecture	17	14
Accounting	14	12
Enjoyable campus		
Yes	103	85
No	18	15

4.2 *Validity and Reliability Testing*

The validity and reliability were tested by PLS through the measurement model (outer model). The measurement model was evaluated by examining the individual loadings of each item which are called internal composite reliability (ICR) and average variance extracted (AVE) per variable to test validity of variables (Chin 1998; Roostika 2011). Thus, The PLS analysis produces composite reliability measure which is similar to Cronbach's alpha, but preferred in structural equations modeling because it estimates consistency on the basis of actual measurement loadings. The internal consistency values should exceed the 0.60 (Roostika 2011).

Table 2 indicates that all of the variables fit with the requirements such as AVE that are greater than 0.5 (Chin 1998; Ghozali 2006) and each of the variables contains ICR which are more than 0.6 (Chin 1998; Fornell and Lacker 1998). Thus, Table 2 informed that each of the items has significant t-value at the $p < 0.001$ level (T-statistics > 1.96) which is confirmed the statistical requirement stated earlier. Table 2 also confirmed that each of the variables containing Cronbach Alpha which is greater than 0.7. It is concluded that this study meet the requirements of validity and reliability as required by PLS analysis.

Table 2 Validity and reliability testing

Variables	Indicators	Standardized loading factor	T-statistics	Internal composite reliability (ICR)	Average variance extracted (AVE)	Cronbach alpha
Expectation disconfirmation (McKnight 2005)	edt1	0.80744	19.302322	0.940023	0.691402	0.925472
	edt2	0.848164	19.572979			
	edt3	0.853296	20.387793			
	edt4	0.847746	19.977288			
	edt5	0.795021	14.450056			
	edt6	0.843507	18.637929			
	edt7	0.823484	23.095989			
Students' Satisfaction (Naik et al. 2010)	cs1	0.852964	20.950148	0.918507	0.738103	0.881689
	cs2	0.843612	24.056075			
	cs3	0.864857	26.726822			
	cs4	0.874759	21.856603			
University image (Kazoleas et al. 2001)	ui1	0.882352	19.004578	0.910235	0.717215	0.86848
	ui2	0.876396	23.82421			
	ui3	0.880798	21.378906			
	ui4	0.831073	17.258349			
E-WoM (Mikalef et al. 2013)	ewom1	0.832305	14.805649	0.924272	0.753276	0.890623
	ewom2	0.842942	14.870003			
	ewom3	0.87804	19.100939			
	ewom4	0.833441	15.07163			

4.3 Hypothesis Testing

To test the hypothesis, PLS analysis required the structural model (inner model) to be assessed by examining the path coefficients, t-statistics and R2 value (Chin 1988; Roostika 2011; Nelloh and Liem 2012).

At the first, hypothesis 1 proposed that expectation disconfirmation (EDT) significantly and positively effect on students' satisfaction by seeing path coefficient and T-statistics through Figs. 1 and 2. Figure 2 concluded that expectation disconfirmation significantly and positively effect on students' satisfaction (t = 47.649) which is greater than statistical requirement (>1.96) it is related to Bhattacherjee and Premkumar (2004) which is stated that EDT will impact on Overall satisfaction is understood as customer's satisfaction of previous purchase experience from websites that such a satisfaction can include all different aspects, like: customer's information satisfaction, online facilities satisfaction, and purchase satisfaction.

Thus Fig. 1 concluded that 0.888 is the path coefficient between expectation disconfirmation toward students' satisfaction. Expectation disconfirmation explained students' satisfaction by 78.9 %. Figure 2 also explained path coefficient of students' satisfaction toward university image containing 0.848 as stated in hypothesis 2. University image is explained by students' satisfaction by 71.8 %. Thus, hypothesis 2 is accepted by seeing the T-statistics = 29.605 it is related to balance theory (Helm et al. 2007) which is previously explained that if the students experienced the university through their satisfaction of the university then students will have a good reputation on the university. Furthermore, hypothesis 3 is accepted with T-statistics = 21.877 (university image toward E-WoM).

Figure 1 concluded that university image explain E-WoM by 61 %. It supported the results of previous studies by Jiewanto et al. (2012) that concluded that if the students have a good reputation or image of the university then they tend to spread good news about the university to the society. Hence, it is related to study of Mikalef et al. (2013) which is resulting on electronic word-of-mouth intention.

5 Conclusion

The main objective of the present study is to measure EDT and university image and to prevent E-WoM influence by focusing on students' satisfaction. Previous research stated that E-WoM is more influential than firm-generated information (Bickart and Schinder 2001) so, actively making efforts to stimulate and manage E-WoM is needed. Therefore, it is extremely important for both academics and practitioners to understand how E-WoM works. In this paper, the authors have demonstrated that happy or delight feeling affects on how students say about the university. Students feeling should be maintained since it affects the way they study.

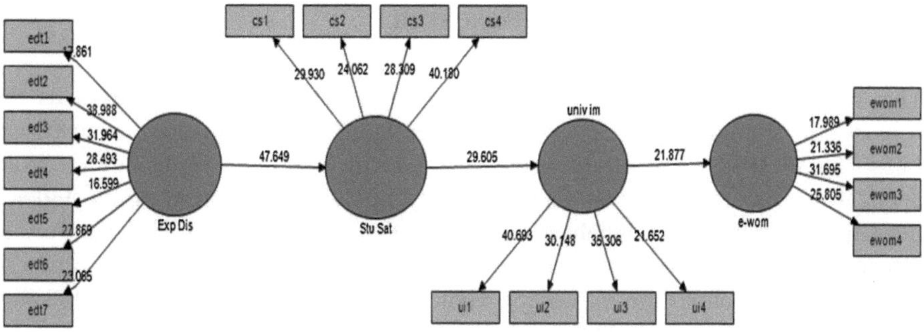

Fig. 5 Structural model (T-statistics)

Since EDT is significantly and positively affect on students satisfactions, and students' satisfaction will influence on how high E-WoM would be for creating university image, as a result image will affect customers' decision making (Fig. 5). Additionally, university should bear in mind that E-WoM has a great impact on customer behavior. Special attention should be devoted to students' satisfaction. Students' satisfaction should be constantly monitored in order to identify problem areas and make necessary improvement and modifications. These actions will enhance students' satisfaction so as to generate positive EDT with positive E-WoM.

6 Research Implications

There are some implications of this research including theoretical implications and managerial implications. For theoretical implications, EDT is significantly applied in the university context. Herewith, the academician should aware that EDT is one of the important antecedents of student satisfaction and university image. This research also confirmed balance theory as proposed by Helm et al. (2007) as the part of visa versa relationship between university image or reputation and student satisfaction. Thus, this research proved nowadays, electronic word-of-mouth to be the important factor in the perspectives of academic entrepreneurship.

For managerial implications, since this research confirmed four hypotheses, then the researchers suggested the head of institutions at entrepreneurial university should consider about expectation disconfirmation toward the students. The managerial should consider the marketing department and all the people included in the university to make an honest and professional promotion toward the students or parents in order to avoid over promising to them. Furthermore, as the result of this research, the managerial should consider about making an interactive social media promotion, increasing the viral marketing or referral through the internet so that existing students will have positive perceived image and or satisfied toward the university. Hence, the entrepreneurial university should build its own branding strategy to elaborate the emotional or affective sources of the students.

7 Limitations and Future Research

This research contains some limitations. Firstly, the number of students as the respondents should be more elaborated. Even though it is avoided by using Partial Least Square (PLS), the future research should include more students as respondents. Thus, this research only focuses on psychological or mindset of the students does not include the real behavior as word-of-mouth behavior. So, the further research should include more variables such as university service quality in order to test subjectively about the university. Hence, the future research include not only from behavioral intentions but also behavioral actions of the students.

References

Bearden WO, Teel JE (1993) Some determinants of consumer of satisfaction and complaints reports. J Mark Res 21–28

Bhattacherjee A, Premkumar G (2004) Understanding changes in belief and attitude toward information technology usage: a theoretical model and longitudinal test. MIS

Bickart B, Schindler R (2001) Internet forums as influential sources of consumer information. J Interact Mark 35–40

Brown J, Dacin P (1997) The company and the product: corporate associations and consumer product responses. J Mark 61:68–84

Brown TJ, Dacin K (1999) The influence of pre-encounter affect on satisfaction with an anxiety-provoking service encounter. Serv Res Policy 333–346

Chin WW (1998) The partial least square approach to structural equation modeling. In: Marcoulides Ga (ed) Modern methods for business research. Lawrence Erlbaum Associates, Mahwah, London, New Jersey, pp 295–336

Chin WW, Marcolin B, Newsted P (2003) A partial least squares latent variable modeling approach for measuring interaction effects: results from a monte carlo simulation study and an electronic-mail emotion/adoption Study. Inf Syst Res 14(2):189–217

Chu S-C (2009) Determinants of consumer engagement in electronic word-of-mouth in social networking sites. PhD Dissertation, University of Texas, Austin

Churchill GA, Surprenant C (1982) An investigation into the determinants of consumer satisfaction. J Mark Res 491–504

Ghorban ZS, Tahernejad H (2012) A study on effect of brand credibility on word of mouth: with reference to internet service providers in Malaysia. Int J Mark Stud 4(1), Feb 2012

Ghozali I (2006) Structural equation modeling. Metode Alternatif dengan PLS, Badan Penerbit Undip, Semarang

Goldsmith RE, Horowitz D (2006) Measuring motivations for online opinion seeking. J Interact Advertising 6(2):3–14

Hair JF, Black WC, Babin BJ, Anderson RE (2010) Multivariate data analysis, 7th edn. Pearson, Upper Saddle River

Harian Medan Bisnis (2015) http://www.medanbisnisdaily.com. Accessed 11 March 2015

Haistead D, Hartman D (1994) Multisource effects on the satisfaction formation process. Acad Mark Sci 114–129

Helm S, Spelsiek J, Garnefeld I (2007) Perceived corporate reputation and consumer satisfaction: an experimental exploration of causal relationships. http://anzmac.org/conference_archive/2007/papers/S%20Helm_1a.pdf

Hennig-Thurau T, Walsh G (2004) Electronic word of mouth: motives for and consequences for reading customer articulations on the Internet. Int J Electron Commer 8(2):51–74

Jawa Pos National Network (2014) http://www.jpnn.com/. Accessed 13 July 2015

Jiewanto A, Laurens C, Nelloh L (2012) Influence of service quality, university image, and student satisfaction toward WOM intention: a case study on Universitas Pelita Harapan Surabaya. International Conference on Asia Pacific Business Innovation and Technology Management. 1877-0428 © 2012, Published by Elsevier Ltd

Kaplan AM, Haenlein M (2010) Users of the world, unite! The challenges and opportunities of social media

Kazoleas D, Kim Y, Moffit MA (2001) Institutional image: a case study. Corp Commun: Int J 6:205–216

Kompas L (2015) http://www.mri-research-ind.com/berita-249-wirausaha-indonesia-tertinggal-jauh.html. Accessed 10 Aug 2015

Lee J, Park, Han I (2008) The effect of negative online consumer reviews on product attitude: an information processing view

Lewicki RJ, Buncker BB (eds) (1996) Trust in relationships: a model of trust development and decline. Conflict, Cooperation and Justice. Jossey-Bass, San Fransisco Jossey-Bass

Martenson R (2007) Corporate brand image, satisfaction and store loyalty: a study of the store as a brand, store brands and manufacturer brands. Int J Retail Distrib Manage 35(7):544–555. doi:10.1108/09590550710755921

McKnight DH (2005) Trust in information technology. In: Davis GB (ed) The Blackwell encyclopedia of management, vol 7., Management information systems BlackwellMalden, MA, pp 329–331

Mikalef P, Giannakos M, Pateli A (2013) Shopping and word-of-mouth intentions on social media. J Theo Appl Electron Commer Res 8(1) ISSN 0718-1876 Electronic Version. Apr 2013

Naik CN, Krishna SB, Gantasala G, Prabhakar V (2010) Servqual, customer satisfaction and behavioural intentions in retailing. Eur J Soc Sci 17(2)

Nelloh L, Jiewanto A (2012) Students attitudes and trust toward university: the importance university of ethics and value in UPH surabaya. World Rev Bus Res 2(3):174–190

Nelloh L, Liem CCP (2012) Analisis Switching Intention Penggunaan Jasa Layanan Rumah Kos di Siwalankerto: Perspektif Kualitas Layanan dan Kepuasan Pelanggan. Jurnal Manajemen Pemasaran, 6(1), ISSN 1907235X

Oliver RL (1977) Effect of expectation and disconfirmation on postexposure product evaluations: an alternative interpretation. J Appl Psychol 480–486

Oliver RL (1989) A cognitive model for antecedents and consequences of satisfaction. J Mark Res 17:460–469

Phelps et al (2004) Viral marketing or word-of-mouth advertising: examining consumer responses and motivations to pass along email. J Advertising Res 333–348

Roostika R (2011) The effect of perceived service quality and trust on loyalty. customer's perspectives on mobile internet adoption. Int J Innov, Manage Technol 2(4)

Santos J, Boote J (2003) A theoretical exploration and model of consumer expectations, post purchase affective states and affective behavior. J Consum Behav 142–156

Sevier RA (1994) Image is everything: strategies for measuring, changing, and maintaining your institution's image

Sheridan TB (1988) Trustworthiness of command and control systems. Proceedings of the 3rd IFAC conference on analysis, design and evaluation of man-machine systems, Oulu, Finland, pp 427–431

Smith et al (2007) Online peer and editorial recommendations, trust and choice in virtual markets. J Interact Mark 19(3):5–37

Spreng RA, MacKenzie SB (1996) A reexamination of the determinants of consumer satisfaction. J Mark 15–32

Tse DK, Wilton PC (1998) Models of consumer satisfaction formation: an extension. J Mark Res 25:204–212

Yi Y (1990) A critical review of consumer satisfaction. In: Zeithaml VA (ed) Review of marketing. American Marketing Association, Chicago, pp 68–123

Large Controlling Shareholder, Corporate Governance, and Cross-Border M&A Decision: An Empirical Study Based on Listed Companies in China

Kai Liu and Chaohong Na

Abstract Based on domestic M&A and cross-border M&A events in China from 2007 to 2013, we investigate the large shareholder's agency problem on domestic and cross-border M&A decision-making, then analyze the governance effects of internal and external governance mechanism on the agency problem.The results show that large shareholder's agency problem exists in the Chinese listed company's cross-border M&A decision-making, the SOE or large shareholder are unwilling to carry out cross-border M&A. Further study found that, the equity balance degree, the international background of board chairman, and foreign sales level can alleviate the equity agency problem on cross-border M&A, but the product market competition will aggravate the equity agency problems on cross-border M&A. This paper complements and expands the cross-border M&A theory, provides a theoretical and empirical evidence to formulate relevant M&A policies for regulators and to promote the internationalization strategy for listed companies in China.

Keywords Cross-border M&A · Large controlling shareholder · Agency problem · Corporate governance

1 Introduction

In recent years, driven by rapid economic growth, the Chinese economy is changing from bringing into going out and from product exporting to capacity transferring and capital outputting. China's M&A market shows a trend of explosive growth, the listed companies have to optimize the allocation of resources, expand the scale

K. Liu (✉)
School of Economics and Management, China University of Petroleum, Qingdao, China
e-mail: jnukk@163.com

C. Na
School of Accounting, Yunnan University of Finance and Economics, Kunming, China
e-mail: ausman@263.net

S. Soh (ed.), *Selected Papers from the Asia Conference on Economics & Business Research 2015*, DOI 10.1007/978-981-10-0986-0_5

of enterprises, achieve strategic transformation and accelerate the internationalization process by M&A, both the number and the size of the transaction increase sharply, cross-border M&A accounts for more than half of the total transaction volume, compared with domestic M&A, which is more conducive for listed companies to acquire the key assets like brand, market, technology, and management skills, to enhance their international competitiveness, and to make more positive effects on the future innovations (Bena and Kai 2014). It has become an important tool for the implementation of international strategy in china. However, due to the complexity of integration after the merger, and the lack of enterprise innovation and multinational management ability, the difficulty and risk of cross-border M&A is much higher than domestic M&A. Cross-border M&A only accounts for about 10 % of the total number of M&A, so there exists the problem on insufficient power of cross-border M&A. With the deepening of the internationalization and cross-border M&A gaining a more and more important position in the market, the primary problem which Chinese listed companies need to solve in order to increase international competitiveness is how to guide and promote the implementation of cross-border M&A effectively. Therefore, research on the key drivers of cross-border M&A has very important practical significance.

Many scholars have done lots of researches, using Chinese enterprises cross-border M&A as the research object, and have achieved abundant results, separately on M&A motivation (Xianming and Zhiwen 2014), the factors influencing M&A implementation success or failure (Jianhong et al. 2010), overseas expansion mode (Qinqin and Yanyan 2014) and whether M&A can create values, and decision factors of value creation (Lulu and Robert 2011),while the studies of cross-border M&A decision-making are limited.

In view of this, using 2066 M&A events of Chinese listed companies from 2007 to 2013, based on agency theory, this paper introduces the large controlling shareholder in the study of cross-border M&A decision-making, and further analyze large shareholder's agency problem on cross-border M&A decision-making and the governance effect of internal and external governance mechanism, from the internal and external governance factors reflecting the "intention" and "ability" of the cross-border M&A, so as to provide empirical support to enrich cross-border M&A decision-making theory and guide listed companies advance the strategy of internationalization actively and steadily.

2 Literature Review and Research Hypothesis

Due to the particularity of Chinese institutional environment, in recent years, scholars began to introduce company internal and external governance factors, such as equity structure, board governance, and product's market competition into the M&A decision-making research. However, most study use domestic M&A events as the research object, and they generally believe that the internal governance structure of listed companies and the external governance environment will directly or indirectly affect the M&A decision-making (Bing et al. 2011). While in the research field of the company internationalization drivers, scholars mainly use the theory of institutional factors and organizational learning to explain how the domestic institutional environment, industry environment and the enterprises' learning ability influence the companies' internationalization process, selection of the overseas investment mode, and implementation effects of cross-border M&A (Deng 2009; Jianhong et al. 2012). The above research all show that company governance factors will affect the M&A decision-making and internationalization, but they fail to study the driving factors of the listed companies' M&A decision-making from a micro perspective of the company internal and external governance mechanism, which can reflect the listed companies' intention and ability to implement cross-border M&A. Therefore, this paper tries to base on the agency theory, from the perspective of company governance, and disclose the "black box" of cross-border M&A decision-making.

2.1 Large Shareholder's Agency Problem in the Cross-border M&A Decision-making

A large number of documents show that the nature of the ultimate controller is the key factor, which influence the process of internationalization and the effect of cross-border M&A. Viewing from the domestic policy environment, on the one hand, SOE's good relations with the government are helpful to obtain the relevant support from industrial policies and finance, and also have a greater competitive advantage in system and industrial environment, compared with the private listed companies (Hui and Shanmin 2011). On other hand, as the domestic M&A market's reform bonus continue to release, SOE behave very actively in the domestic M&A events. But as the cross-border M&A is a high-risk investment, SASAC introduce several policies to strictly examine, approve, and supervise SOE's cross-border M&A events, in order to control the investment risk and realize the preservation and appreciation of the state-owned assets. Such remarkable advantage based on property rights will sharply undermine the SOE's intrinsic motivation to implement the internationalization strategy (Jinhui et al. 2014). Viewing from international environment, in recent years, with the "sinophobia" mood growing in commercial activities, SOE's decision of cross-border M&A is generally considered to be made by government for some political purposes (Ramasamy et al. 2012). Its state-owned identity will cause the host country to worry about the nation security threat and the lack of international management ability. While private listed companies with its flexible autonomous management mechanism and strong ability of international management are favored by foreign enterprises, their cross-border M&A strategies are also viewed as reasonable behaviors to look for the biggest value space of international market. Such international environment will increase the SOE's political cost of cross-border M&A, and constitute the institutional barriers for their implementation of the international strategy. As a result, SOE are inclined to make domestic M&A which has lower risk and higher success rate, taking advantage of the domestic institutional environment. In the corporate governance mode where the company is mainly controlled by large shareholder, the proposal of M&A is basically the will of the large shareholder. Especially in emerging market countries, large shareholder's control and cash flow rights diverge severely, and conspiracy with managers is easy to appear, then decisions which encroach on minority shareholders' benefits will be made, and tunneling effect is obvious here (John 2008). Research has found that large shareholders are more tend to make lower risk investment to obtain more private benefit. Because large shareholders in emerging market countries lack experience of transitional operation and deep understanding of oversea market, internationalization usually bring high risk and high cost. As a result, they are not willing to enter the more complex oversea market, and at the same time force their CEO to make investment decisions which avoid risks. The above discussion leads to our first hypothesis:

H_1 company has large shareholder agency problem on cross-border M&A decision-making.

H_{1a} SOE are more unwilling to carry out cross-border M&A.

H_{1b} listed company with higher large shareholder's ownership proportion is more unwilling to carry out cross-border M&A.

2.2 *Governance Effect of the Corporate Governance Mechanism in Equity Agency Problem on Cross-Border M&A Decision-making*

2.2.1 Internal Governance Mechanism

In corporate enterprise with separation of two rights, the large quantities of agency cost are usually caused by performance decline arising from wrong decision. Therefore, improving decision-making efficiency and strengthening supervision mechanism can reduce the enterprise moral hazard and adverse selection behavior.

The board of shareholder is a major factor to supervise the significant decision-making behavior in company under large shareholders' control. In the board of shareholders' governance structure, the other major shareholders of listed companies, unlike the first big shareholders, mainly play the role to supervise, check, and balance big shareholders' behavior. It is a kind of important mechanism to protect the interests of outside investors in this structure. To some extent, the more powerful the other large shareholders are, the more obvious the effect of supervision and checks and balances on its largest shareholder is, the more helpful to alleviate the equity agency problem in cross-border M&A decision-making problem.

In addition to representing the general meeting of shareholders to supervise the management behavior, board of directors' more important job is to provide resources and make strategic decision, in order to improve the efficiency of major investment and financing decision, and take on the role to make an enterprise strategic decision (Liangyong and Xiaoling 2014). In this structure, the board can form an ability complementary effect where many people involved in decision-making, and the greater the board's size is, the more able it is to play a role in important strategic decision-making. Compared with domestic M&A, uncertainty of cross-border M&A makes the decision more difficult, while the strategic behavior of the board has more importance in a more complex investment decision. At the same time, overseas experience of members of the board is helpful to cultivate global thinking mode and cope with the uncertainty of international capital operation, so as to promote the integration of resources on a global scale through cross-border M&A, foster international competitive advantage, and improve the efficiency of cross-border M&A decision-making (Giannetti submitted for publication). Therefore, a greater size of the board and oversea background of the chairman help the company to carry out cross-border M&A, and alleviate large shareholder equity agency problem on cross-border M&A decision-making.

2.2.2 External Governance Environment

Viewing from the industry environment of the company, based on the agency cost theory, product market competition can be seen as its external governance and adjustment mechanism, when the internal governance mechanism is relatively weak. On the one hand, it can alleviate the generally existed agency problem in listed companies. Research has found that product market competition can make positive effect to promote SOE to carry out cross-border M&A. On the other hand, it will urge listed company to carry out cross-border M&A to get rid of the limit and restrain of the fierce domestic competition, and construct international competitive advantages (Chunxiang and Dunli 2013).

Viewing from the international environment, the internationalization usually starts from exporting in domestic companies. From a certain extent, company's overseas sales level can reflect its internationalization degree and represent its "reputation" and "ability" it enjoys in the international market. Also, its internationalization process is a process of constant learning and experience accumulation, which can lower the cost and risk of the cross-border M&A activity (Liang 2012). In examining the role of international relations on China's foreign direct investment, we find that Chinese investors choose to invest in high-risk environment abroad. It is mainly decided by its good international relations, and such a good international environment is conducive to accumulate overseas business experience and reduce the risk of integration after the merger. Therefore, a higher level of overseas sales helps to alleviate the large shareholder agency problem in cross-border M&A decision-making. The above discussion leads to our second hypothesis:

H_2 A good internal governance mechanism and external governance environment can make the company more willing to carry out cross-border M&A, and alleviate large shareholder agency problem on cross-border M&A decision-making.

3 Research Design

3.1 Sample Selection and Data Sources

This paper uses Chinese listed companies which carried out M&A from January 1, 2007 to December 31, 2013 as samples, and chooses Zdatabase and CSMAR merging and reorganization database as the sample source of the Chinese listed company cross-border M&A and domestic M&A data. Company governance data and international background data used in the empirical test are mainly from the CSMAR database. The standards of the sample selection are as follows: (1) Sample companies are A-share listed companies, excluding those from finance and insurance industry and ST company. (2) Date of announcement of the M&A is between January 1, 2007 and December 31, 2013, and the scale of the M&A needs to outnumber 1 % of the company's scale. (3) Several domestic or cross-border M&A events occurring in the same sample and on the same day counts as one event, and if the sample carries out domestic M&A and cross-border M&A on the same date, then this sample should be eliminated. (4) Samples with missing data should be eliminated. Final sample includes 2066 M&A events, with 1877 domestic M&A and 179 cross-border M&A.

3.2 Variable Selection

3.2.1 Explained Variable

Whether this company carries out cross-border M&A is the explained variable in this paper. Number 1 means cross-border M&A, and 0 means domestic M&A.

3.2.2 Explanatory Variable

In this paper, we setup 7 explanatory variables, such as company equity agency problem, company governance structure, and external governance environment variables, and the value of the explanatory variables are the last year's annual report data of the sample before the M&A announcement, which is more conducive to verify the impact of the company's cross-border M&A decision-making.

3.2.3 Control Variable

This paper uses related articles about influencing factors of M&A decision-making as reference, and selects the size of the company, financial leverage, profitability, and growth indicators as control variables. The value of the above control variables are the last year's annual report data of the sample before the M&A announcement, and in the empirical analysis, the industry and the year of the M&A are controlled. The specific definition and measurement of variables are in Table 1.

3.3 Model Specification

As the explained variable in this paper is a binary virtual variable, we choose a binary logistic regression model to test the influencing factors of the listed company's cross-border M&A decision-making.

We set up model 1 to test the large shareholder equity agency problem in listed companies on cross-border M&A decision-making and direct influence of the internal governance mechanism and external governance environment on cross-border M&A decision-making.

$$\begin{aligned}\log[P(MA_{t+1}=1)/P(MA_{t+1}=0)] = \alpha &+ \beta_1 SOE + \beta_2 Top1 + \beta_3 Zind + \beta_4 BSize \\ &+ \beta_5 FExp + \beta_6 FSales + \beta_7 CNum \\ &+ \beta_8 Size + \beta_9 Lev + \beta_{10} Roe + \beta_{11} Q \\ &+ \beta_{12} Grow + \varepsilon_i\end{aligned}$$

We set up model 2 to test whether company governance mechanism will have different governance effect on cross-border M&A decision-making of companies who have different nature of the ultimate controller, introducing separately cross-product term of the nature of the ultimate controller with internal governance variable and the one of the nature with external governance variable. CG represents internal governance variable and external governance variable in the model, and SOE_CG stands for the cross-product term of the nature of ultimate controller with different governance variable separately.

$$\begin{aligned}\log[P(MA_{t+1}=1)/P(MA_{t+1}=0)] = \alpha &+ \beta_1 SOE\_CG + \beta_2 CG + \beta_3 Size \\ &+ \beta_4 Lev + \beta_5 Roe + \beta_6 Q + \beta_7 Grow + \varepsilon_i\end{aligned}$$

We set up model 3 to test whether the sound internal and external governance mechanism can alleviate the large shareholder equity agency problem on cross-border M&A decision-making, keeping the nature of ultimate controller and introducing the cross-product term of the large shareholder's ownership proportion

Table 1 Definition and measurement of variables

Variable type	Variable symbol	Variable definition	Variable measurement
Dependent variable	MA	Whether is cross-border M&A or not	When the sample carries out cross-border M&A, value 1, and when it carries out domestic M&A, value 0
Explanatory variable	Equity agency problem variable		
	SOE	Nature of ultimate controller	When the actual controller is state-owned, value 1, or else value 0
	Top1	Large shareholder's ownership proportion	Largest shareholder stake
	Internal governance structure variable		
	Zind	Equity balance degree	The number of shares of the second largest shareholder divided by the number of shares of the first largest shareholder
	BSize	Board size	Number of the board members
	FExp	Overseas background of the chairman	When the chairman has a foreign nationality or overseas studying or working experience, value 1, or else value 0
	External governance structure variable		
	FSales	Overseas sales level	Company's internationalization degree, 100*overseas sales revenue/total sales revenue
	CNum	Product market competition	Industry competition degree, number of the listed company in the same industry
Control variable	Size	Company scale	Sampling natural logarithm of the company's total assets
	Lev	Asset-liability ratio	Sample company's total debt/total assets
	Roe	Return on equity	Net profit/average net assets
	Q	Tobin's Q	(the market value of equity + the market value of net debt)/final total assets
	Grow	Revenue growth rate	(past year's operation revenue before M&A-past two years' operation revenue)/last two years' operation revenue
	Ind	Industry control variable	Set industry virtual variable according to *Industry classification guidance of listed companies*
	Year	Year control variable	Set year virtual variable when carries out M&A

with equity balance degree, overseas background of chairman, overseas sales level, and product market competition.

$$\log[P(MA_{t+1}=1)/P(MA_{t+1}=0)] = \alpha + \beta_1 SOE + \beta_2 Top1 + \beta_3 Top1\_Zind + \beta_4 Top1\_FExp + \beta_5 Top1\_FSales + \beta_6 Top1\_CNum + \beta_7 Size + \beta_8 Lev + \beta_9 Roe + \beta_{10} Q + \beta_{11} Grow + \varepsilon_i$$

This paper has tested the correlation of the independent variables, and it turns out that all correlation coefficients are lower than 0.5, and the VIF of all models is smaller than 2 at the same time. There is no problem of multi-collinearity.

4 The Empirical Results and Analysis

4.1 Descriptive Statistical Analysis

Table 2 is the results of descriptive statistical analysis of all variables in a complete sample. We can see from the table that the average value of MA is 0.09, which means number of cross-border M&A account for 9 % of number of the whole M&A. Viewing from the proportion of the M&A, proportion of cross-border M&A of listed companies is basically the same as that of all other companies, and this means that samples of cross-border M&A in listed companies have good representativeness throughout the country.

Table 2 Descriptive statistical result of complete sample

Variable	Obs	Mean	Std. Dev.	Min	Max
MA	2066	0.09	0.28	0	1
SOE	2066	0.44	0.50	0	1
Top1	2066	0.36	0.15	0.09	0.75
Zind	2066	0.34	0.29	0.01	0.99
BSize	2066	8.94	1.80	5	15
FExp	2066	0.11	0.31	0	1
FSales	2066	11.44	20.94	0	99.65
CNum	2066	159.97	120.06	15.00	478.00
Size	2066	21.56	1.15	18.73	25.18
Lev	2066	0.42	0.22	0.03	1.06
Roe	2066	0.10	0.11	−0.40	0.47
Q	2066	1.75	1.13	0	7.96
Grow	2066	0.58	2.19	−0.75	17.45

4.2 Single Variable Variance Analysis Results

According to the medians of the nature of ultimate controller reflecting the equity problem and equity of stock holdings, as well as the medians of the chairman's overseas background, equity balance degree, board size, overseas sales level, and product market competition, we divide samples into 7 groups for the average T-test of cross-border M&A decision-making, in order to verify whether there is significant difference.

Table 3 shows that SOE are more unwilling to carry out cross-border M&A, and listed companies with high large shareholder's ownership proportion have weak will too, which is not remarkable. Table 4 shows higher equity balance degree, bigger board size, chairman's overseas background, and higher overseas sales level have positive effect on cross-border M&A decision-making, while higher product market competition degree will restrain cross-border M&A decision-making, which is not obvious. It means that sound internal and external governance mechanism can encourage it to carry out cross-border M&A, while market competition can restrain its willingness to carry out cross-border M&A.

4.3 Test Results of Logistic Regression Model

4.3.1 Test Result of Large Shareholder Equity Agency Problem on Cross-Border M&A Decision-making

Table 5 is the regression result of model 1, and it shows that large shareholders' ownership proportion and nature of ultimate controller have remarkable negative correlation with cross-border M&A decision-making. It means SOE and listed company with higher larger shareholder's ownership proportion are more unwilling to carry out cross-border M&A, and it proves the existence of the large shareholder equity agency problem in cross-border M&A decision-making, which supports for hypothesis H_1. Equity balance degree, chairman's overseas background, and overseas sales level all have remarkable positive correlation with cross-border M&A decision-making, and board size has un remarkable correlation with

Table 3 Difference examination of cross-border M&A decision-making grouped by equity agency problem

Cross-border M&A	Nature of ultimate controller		Large shareholder's ownership proportion	
	State-owned	Private	Higher	Lower
Average	0.068	0.101	0.079	0.093
T-test value	2.657***		1.099	

*, **, and *** denote significance at the 10 %, 5 %, and 1 % level respectively

Table 4 Difference examination of cross-border M&A decision-making grouped by governance variable

Cross-border M&A	Equity balance degree		Board size		Chairman's overseas background		Overseas sales level		Product market competition	
	Higher	Lower	Bigger	Smaller	Yes	No	Higher	Lower	Higher	Lower
Average	0.104	0.069	0.108	0.082	0.159	0.078	0.133	0.040	0.077	0.096
T-test value	2.782***		1.671*		4.129***		7.612***		1.520	

*, **, and *** denote significance at the 10 %, 5 %, and 1 % level respectively

Table 5 Empirical result of model 1

	(1)	(2)	(3)	(4)	(5)	(6)
	MA	MA	MA	MA	MA	MA
SOE	−0.705***	−0.673***	−0.774***	−0.763***	−0.715***	−0.731***
	(−3.34)	(−3.17)	(−3.63)	(−3.62)	(−3.30)	(−3.49)
Top1	−1.017*	–	–	–	–	–
	(−1.83)	–	–	–	–	–
Zind	–	0.773***	–	–	–	–
	–	(2.80)	–	–	–	–
BSize	–	–	0.064	–	–	–
	–	–	(1.30)	–	–	–
FExp	–	–	–	0.728***	–	–
	–	–	–	(3.33)	–	–
FSales	–	–	–	–	0.026***	–
	–	–	–	–	(7.58)	–
CNum	–	–	–	–	–	−0.006**
	–	–	–	–	–	(−2.10)
Size	0.714***	0.696***	0.671***	0.696***	0.728***	0.695***
	(7.32)	(7.20)	(6.87)	(7.20)	(7.31)	(7.22)
Lev	−2.025***	−1.802***	−1.927***	−1.828***	−1.759***	−2.057***
	(−3.85)	(−3.42)	(−3.67)	(−3.45)	(−3.27)	(−3.89)
Roe	2.559***	2.254**	2.351**	2.311**	2.510**	2.342**
	(2.64)	(2.33)	(2.43)	(2.38)	(2.56)	(2.43)
Q	−0.060	−0.030	−0.041	−0.018	0.004	−0.047
	(−0.62)	(−0.32)	(−0.43)	(−0.19)	(0.04)	(−0.49)
Grow	−0.039	−0.042	−0.040	−0.046	−0.044	−0.045
	(−0.62)	(−0.66)	(−0.64)	(−0.73)	(−0.73)	(−0.72)
_cons	−18.301***	−18.604***	−18.340***	−18.364***	−19.226***	−18.112***
	(−8.55)	(−8.69)	(−8.55)	(−8.57)	(−8.76)	(−8.45)
N	2066	2066	2066	2066	2066	2066
pseudo R^2	0.145	0.149	0.144	0.151	0.187	0.146
chi2	177.097	181.371	175.354	183.881	227.977	178.007

*, **, and *** denote significance at the 10 %, 5 %, and 1 % level respectively

cross-border M&A decision-making, so this is partial support for hypothesis H_2. It means that a sound board, board governance mechanism, and overseas governance environment are helpful for cross-border M&A decision-making. Product market competition degree has negative correlation with cross-border M&A decision-making, which does not go with agency cost theory. According to the management risk theory, when domestic competition of the industry is more intense, the management risk it faces is higher (Irvine and Pontiff 2009). But cross-border M&A is different from the general foreign trade or overseas marketing agency, it is a stratified capital operation method. Therefore, this feature makes its integration risk and management cost much higher than other international operation methods and domestic M&A, which will make the management risk increase exponentially when the company is already in a fierce competition, so as to restrain the cross-border M&A decision-making.

4.3.2 Test Result of Governance Effect of Equity Agency Problem on Cross-border M&A Decision-making

Nature of Ultimate Controller, Corporate Governance and Cross-border M&A Decision-making

Table 6 shows the regression result of model 2, and it turns out that large shareholder equity agency problem on cross-border M&A decision-making is quite remarkable in SOE, which will be more unwilling to carry out cross-border M&A with a higher large shareholder's ownership proportion. The cross-product term of the nature of ultimate controller with internal and external governance variable is remarkable negative, which means that sound board governance, shareholders' governance and overseas governance environment have more positive effect on cross-border M&A decision-making in private listed companies, while SOE have poor governance effect on cross-border M&A decision-making. Intense product market competition will remarkably decrease listed company's willingness to carry out cross-border M&A, especially in SOE.

Large Shareholder's Ownership Proportion, Corporate Governance, and Cross-border M&A Decision-making

Table 7 shows the regression result of model 3, and it turns out that the cross-product terms of large shareholder's ownership proportion with equity balance degree, chairman's overseas background and overseas sales level all have positive correlation with cross-border M&A decision-making. This means that sound board, board governance mechanism, and overseas governance environment are conducive to improve large shareholder's enthusiasm to carry out cross-border M&A and alleviate the equity agency problem. While the cross-product term of large shareholder's ownership proportion with product market competition is negative, explained by management risk theory, the fiercer the industry competition is, large shareholders are more unwilling to carry out cross-border M&A with high risk, in order to avoid risks. As a result, product market competition environment cannot be an effective external governance mechanism of cross-border M&A decision-making, while in turn it will aggravate large shareholder equity agency problem. So it partially support hypothesis H_2.

The regression coefficients and statistical indicators of control variables in Tables 5, 6, and 7 all show that company size and ROE have remarkable positive

Table 6 Empirical result of model 2

	(1) MA	(2) MA	(3) MA	(4) MA	(5) MA	(6) MA
SOE _ Top1	−1.515***	–	–	–	–	–
	(−2.94)	–	–	–	–	–
Top1	−0.452	–	–	–	–	–
	(−0.77)	–	–	–	–	–
SOE_Zind	–	−1.051**	–	–	–	–
	–	(−2.53)	–	–	–	–
Zind	–	1.226***	–	–	–	–
	–	(4.09)	–	–	–	–
SOE_BSize	–	–	−0.080***	–	–	–
	–	–	(−3.60)	–	–	–
BSize	–	–	0.104**	–	–	–
	–	–	(2.00)	–	–	–
SOE_FExp	–	–	–	−0.525	–	–
	–	–	–	(−1.26)	–	–
FExp	–	–	–	0.899***	–	–
	–	–	–	(3.36)	–	–
SOE_FSales	–	–	–	–	−0.017***	–
	–	–	–	–	(−2.83)	–
FSales	–	–	–	–	0.032***	–
	–	–	–	–	(8.12)	–
SOE_CNum	–	–	–	–	–	−0.002*
	–	–	–	–	–	(−1.74)
CNum	–	–	–	–	–	−0.006**
	–	–	–	–	–	(−2.11)
Size	0.701***	0.670***	0.665***	0.604***	0.670***	0.625***
	(7.18)	(7.04)	(6.84)	(6.56)	(7.05)	(6.69)
Lev	−2.092***	−1.909***	−1.972***	−1.991***	−1.808***	−2.116***
	(−4.00)	(−3.64)	(−3.76)	(−3.81)	(−3.40)	(−4.03)
Roe	2.553***	2.438**	2.343**	2.609***	2.817***	2.519***
	(2.62)	(2.54)	(2.42)	(2.74)	(2.92)	(2.64)
Q	−0.061	−0.040	−0.043	−0.048	−0.022	−0.061
	(−0.62)	(−0.42)	(−0.45)	(−0.50)	(−0.22)	(−0.63)
Grow	−0.041	−0.041	−0.040	−0.045	−0.043	−0.042
	(−0.64)	(−0.65)	(−0.64)	(−0.73)	(−0.71)	(−0.68)
_cons	−18.280***	−18.354***	−18.529***	−16.664***	−18.310***	−16.919***
	(−8.43)	(−8.58)	(−8.57)	(−8.04)	(−8.59)	(−8.01)
N	2066	2066	2066	2066	2066	2066
pseudo R^2	0.143	0.146	0.144	0.141	0.185	0.138
chi2	174.244	177.646	174.904	171.625	225.149	168.381

*, **, and *** denote significance at the 10 %, 5 %, and 1 % level respectively

Table 7 Empirical result of model 3

	(1)	(2)	(3)	(4)	(5)
	MA	MA	MA	MA	MA
SOE	−0.714***	−0.775***	−0.749***	−0.768***	−0.761***
	(−3.38)	(−3.67)	(−3.47)	(−3.65)	(−3.48)
Top1	−0.737	−1.352**	−2.243***	0.595	−0.764
	(−1.30)	(−2.40)	(−3.71)	(0.68)	(−0.80)
Top1_Zind	2.348**	–	–	–	2.167**
	(2.23)	–	–	–	(2.02)
Top1_FExp	–	2.021***	–	–	1.173**
	–	(3.79)	–	–	(2.01)
Top1_FSales	–	–	0.056***	–	0.051***
	–	–	(6.97)	–	(6.17)
Top1_CNum	–	–	–	−0.009**	−0.008*
	–	–	–	(−2.30)	(−1.92)
Size	0.697***	0.711***	0.751***	0.706***	0.737***
	(7.34)	(7.42)	(7.63)	(7.42)	(7.42)
Lev	−1.670***	−1.780***	−1.743***	−1.873***	−1.465***
	(−3.16)	(−3.39)	(−3.29)	(−3.60)	(−2.70)
Roe	2.451**	2.742***	2.772***	2.839***	2.480**
	(2.52)	(2.82)	(2.84)	(2.95)	(2.49)
Q	−0.031	−0.048	−0.033	−0.077	−0.001
	(−0.32)	(−0.50)	(−0.34)	(−0.79)	(−0.01)
Grow	−0.041	−0.043	−0.039	−0.040	−0.040
	(−0.65)	(−0.67)	(−0.62)	(−0.63)	(−0.64)
_cons	−18.319***	−18.195***	−18.845***	−18.606***	−19.238***
	(−8.77)	(−8.64)	(−8.79)	(−8.79)	(−8.86)
N	2066	2066	2066	2066	2066
pseudo R^2	0.164	0.171	0.198	0.165	0.207
chi2	206.433	214.665	248.514	207.115	260.498

*, **, and *** denote significance at the 10 %, 5 %, and 1 % level respectively

correlation with cross-border M&A decision-making, while asset-liability ratio has negative correlation with cross-border M&A decision-making. This means listed company with large scale, high profitability, and low debt levels are more inclined to carry out cross-border M&A for its stronger anti-risk capacity.

5 Conclusion and Revelation

This paper empirically tested large shareholder equity agency problem on cross-border M&A decision-making, and further analyzed the governance effect of board, board governance mechanism, and external governance environment on equity agency problem in cross-border M&A decision-making. The results have shown, first, equity agency problem does exist on cross-border M&A decision-making, and SOE and large shareholder are unwilling to carry out cross-border M&A. Second, high equity degree, chairman's overseas background, and high overseas sales level will impel cross-border M&A decision-making and will help large shareholders to make scientific decisions in an effective balance mechanism, alleviate large shareholder equity agency problem and remarkably improve large shareholder's enthusiasm to carry out cross-border M&A. Third, higher equity balance degree, bigger board size, chairman's overseas background, and higher overseas sales level have poor governance effect on cross-border M&A decision-making in SOE, while they have stronger governance effect in private listed companies. Finally, high product market competition degree has negative effect on cross-border M&A decision-making, and high management risk caused by industry competition restrains listed companies' willingness to carry out cross-border M&A and aggravate large shareholder equity agency problem on cross-border M&A decision-making.

In the current environment where our country pushes forward "going out" strategy, to improve listed companies to carry out cross-border M&A, the conclusion above has the following revelation: first of all, Chinese listed companies should consistently improve internal governance structure like shareholders' meeting and board of directors. On the one hand, they should form the corresponding supervision and checks and balances mechanism in large shareholder controlling governance mode, in order to reduce the occurrence of opportunistic M&A. On the other hand, they should constantly improve the ability of scientific decision-making and cross-border management, in order to reduce the risk after the cross-border M&A. In the next place, in order to solve the listed companies' insufficient power problem in fierce industry competition, government should promote domestic mergers and reorganization of such industry, forming an orderly competition between enterprises and sharply increasing superior companies' competitiveness and anti-risk capacities. Accumulation of experience and improvement of strength in M&A can improve companies' enthusiasm to increase international competitive advantage through M&A. Finally, Companies should speed up the construction of international management team, by combination of bringing in international talents and top management going out, in order to enhance the company's international vision and improve scientific decision-making ability. At the same time, companies can accumulate international management experience by establishing overseas branch and sales net to improve the ability and level of cross-border M&A, and finally realize the global resource and market allocation and improve the value of the company.

Acknowledgments This paper is supported by the following research projects. The National Natural Science Foundation of China (Grant No.: 71462031), The Ministry of Education of Humanities and Social Science Project (Grant No.: 12YJA630092), 2015 Qingdao Social Science Fund Project (Grant No.: QDSKL150427), and The Fundamental Research Funds for the Central Universities (Grant No.: 14CX04032B).

Notes on contributors: Kai Liu is a lecture of School of Economics and Management of China University of Petroleum, P.R. China. She is also a doctor in financial management. She is interested in enterprise merger and acquisition. Chaohong Na is an associate professor of School of Accounting and director of Institute of Corporate Finance of Yunnan University of Finance and Economics, and assistant researcher at the China Europe International Business School. He is also a doctor in financial management. He is interested in enterprise merger and acquisition and corporate governance.

References

Bena J, Kai L (2014) Corporate innovations and mergers and acquisitions. J Finance 69(5): 1923–1960
Bing G, Wei L, Ying Z (2011) Company governance, experience learning and continuous M&A—based on the empirical evidence of our country listed company M&A decision-making. J Finance Econ
Chunxiang Z, Dunli Z (2013) Research in relationship between managements' power and company investment under market competition. Acc Res
Deng P (2009) Why do Chinese firms tend to acquire strategic assets in international expansion. J World Bus 44(1):74–84
Giannetti M, Guanmin L, Xiaoyun Y The brain gain of corporate boards: a natural experiment from China. J Finance (submitted for publication)
Hui Y, Shanmin L (2011) Large shareholder status, property right attribute and control benefit obtaining—based on analysis of major equity deal. J Finance Econ
Irvine P, Pontiff J (2009) Idiosyncratic return volatility, cash flows, and product market competition. Rev Financial Stud 22(3):1149–1177
Jianhong Z, Shunqi G, Chaohong Z (2012) Impact of industry characteristics on the process of internationalization—take cross-border M&A as an example. Nankai Econ Stud
Jianhong Z, Xinjiang W, Haike E (2010) Analysis of decision factor of Chinese companies' cross-border success. Management world
Jinhui L, Wei Z, Xiafei X. (2014) Whether the government background hindered the enterprises to carry out the strategy of internationalization. J Shanxi Finance Econ Univ
John K, Litov L, Yeung B (2008) Corporate governance and risk-taking. J Finance 63(4): 1679–1728
Liang X, Lu X, Wang L (2012) Outward internationalization of private enterprises in China. J World Bus 46(1):134–144
Liangyong W, Xiaoling Z (2014) The characteristics of structural holes of the director net and company mergers and acquisitions. Acc Res
Lulu C, Robert R (2011) Does China fail in cross-border M&A? Econ Res J
Qinqin C, Yanyan L (2014) Game analysis of selection of Chinese bank overseas expansion mode. J Finance Econ
Ramasamy B, Yeung M, Laforet S (2012) China's outward foreign direct investment: location choice and firm ownership. J World Bus 47(1):17–25
Xianming W, Zhiwen S (2014) Use cross-border M&A as leverage to catch up technology: perspective of dynamic capability. Management world

Forecasting Patent Filings at the European Patent Office (EPO) with a Dynamic Log Linear Regression Model: Applications and Extensions

Peter Hingley and Walter Park

Abstract We describe the application of a structural econometric model to forecast annual and quarterly total filings of patents at the EPO, amid cyclical shocks. Such models are applicable for national, regional, and international patent offices for budgetary planning purposes. We also provide out-of-sample forecasts out to 2019. The exercise predicts strong further growth in EPO filings from China. The forecasts appear largely optimistic out to 2019. Other findings are that quarterly data do not exhibit as much sensitivity to cyclical influences as do annual data, consistent with the view that innovation decisions are made based upon longer term factors. Furthermore, filings respond more directly to market fluctuations rather than indirectly to deviations in research and development (R&D) spending from trend. The estimates also vary by technological field. Further possibilities for an extension of the approach are discussed, including the usage of country-to-country correlations of forecasts to unearth communalities in patenting behaviour between countries.

Keywords Total filings (Euro-direct filings plus Euro-PCT international phase filings) · Lognormality · Business cycles · Gross domestic product (GDP) · Patent offices · Research and development expenditure (R&D) · Linear model · Variance

1 Introduction

Planners at the European Patent Office (EPO) make forecasts for future patent filings in order to power business planning for all the major points of the patent granting process, such as searches, substantive examinations, grants and renewals.

P. Hingley
European Patent Office, Munich, Germany
e-mail: phingley@epo.org

W. Park (✉)
American University, Washington D.C., USA
e-mail: wgp@american.edu

S. Soh (ed.), *Selected Papers from the Asia Conference on Economics & Business Research 2015*, DOI 10.1007/978-981-10-0986-0_6

There is an annual cycle that proceeds from the forecasts via the business plan that is finalised in a budget document (Hingley and Nicolas 2006). Academic scholars are interested in patent forecasts in order to better understand the determinants of innovation and productivity, which are fundamental influences on economic growth and human progress.

The purpose of this study is to model EPO filings behaviour and derive the implications for forecasting EPO filings out-of-sample, over the medium and longer term. The motivation for this is a study on forecasting EPO filings by Park (2006), in which only long term trends were taken into account. The report was conducted amid an economic boom around the world, driven by the housing market, relatively low energy prices, and the expansion of multinational firm activity, such as outsourcing and offshoring, particularly by the leading technology companies. The earlier study did not anticipate, nor allow for, the effects of a major economic downturn that has come to be known as the *Great Recession*. Consequently Park (2006) produced rather optimistic projections of real gross domestic product (GDP) and EPO filing activity. Instead, there were decreases in EPO filings by leading source countries, like the U.S., Japan, and Germany, particularly in 2009, the critical year of the Great Recession. Thus, business fluctuations seem to have some effect on patenting. However, there also was a relatively quick recovery in filings during 2010–2011. Moreover, for the other countries, their patent filings changed relatively little during the period of the global financial crisis. China's filings actually rose during the Great Recession period. Thus, this raises the issue of how significantly business fluctuations affect patenting and matter to forecasts of future patenting. What is the direction of effect: is patenting pro-cyclical (moves positively with business cycles) or counter-cyclical (moves inversely with business cycles)? How much do business cycles really contribute to changes in patenting? How lasting are the effects of business cycle shocks on patenting? What is the value-added of forecasting business cycles to forecasting EPO filings and applications?

A variety of econometric regression based approaches exist.[1] One of those methods will be considered here, that is based on a dynamic log-linear model (see Hingley and Park 2015a; Park 2006). In an endeavour to improve the model, a business cycles component has been included to supplement trend GDP.

Business cycles refer to fluctuations of output around some average or long run trend path. The trend path of output is usually determined by productivity, technology, or resources. The deviations of output from trend are usually due to nominal shocks, such as aggregate demand shifts in the presence of wage and price rigidities. The reason business cycles are a concern is that when output is below trend, resources are underutilized and unemployment may increase. When output is above trend, inflationary pressures tend to arise. However, there is much debate

[1] See Hingley and Nicolas (2004, 2006), Hidalgo and Gabaly (2012), and Meade (2006) for historical data analyses and European Patent Office (2013) for the survey approach.

about how long lasting business cycles are. One school of thought (for example, the old-Chicago school) is that markets self-correct relatively quickly and that most of the output fluctuations are equilibrium movements or shifts in trend output itself. Another school (for example, the old-Keynesian school) is that economies experience persistent disequilibria. The findings in this chapter present a view that is intermediate between these two schools: output deviations from trend are neither permanent nor equilibrium phenomena.

The chapter is organized as follows. The next section outlines our empirical framework. Section 3 presents estimates of the model and some out-of-sample forecasts. Section 4 re-examines the model from some alternative perspectives, and Sect. 5 discusses other applications. Section 6 concludes. Overall, the study demonstrates the desirability and feasibility of forecasting EPO patent filings under uncertainty about future movements in GDP or the market outlook. The significance is that, to the extent that innovation activities are attuned to market conditions, market fluctuations should affect the capacities and incentives to seek patent protection. Furthermore, the frequency of cycles matters. EPO filings are affected by business cycles when yearly data are considered. For shorter data frequencies—namely quarter to quarter—EPO filings are not as sensitive to business fluctuations. A reason discussed is that significant innovation decisions are not likely to be made on the basis of short-lived circumstances. But on a yearly scale, fluctuations can affect budgetary and other cost factors that impinge upon innovation plans.

2 Empirical Framework

The following regression model is used for EPO filings from a source country:

$$\ln\frac{P}{L} = \alpha_0 + \alpha_1 \ln\left(\frac{P}{L}\right)_{-1} + \alpha_2 \ln\left(\frac{P}{L}\right)_{-2} + \alpha_3 \ln\frac{R}{L} + \alpha_4 \ln\frac{Y^T}{L} + \alpha_5\, u + \varepsilon$$

where P is the number of EPO filings filed by a source country,[2] L is the number of workers in the source country,[3] subscripts −1 and −2 indicate lags of one year and two years respectively, R is R&D expenditures,[4] usually lagged by 5 years, and ε is

[2]EPO filings refers to the sum of Euro-direct and Patent Cooperation Treaty (PCT) international phase filings (see Hingley and Nicolas 2006), excluding divisional filings. Euro-direct are obtained from the EPO production database and PCT are as reported by the World Intellectual Property Organization (WIPO).

[3]Number of workers data are provided by the World Bank *World Development Indicators*: http://data.worldbank.org/data-catalog/world-development-indicators.

[4]R&D expenditures are business enterprise research and development expenditures (BERD) from OECD MSTI 2013 edition 2 (see OECD 2014), at constant 2005 PPP international dollars. Comparable data are taken from UNESCO for countries that are not given by MSTI.

an error term, assumed to be normal with constant variance. ln denotes natural logarithm. The GDP of the source country (Y) is split into two components: Y^T the "trend" level of output, and u a business cycle indicator (namely, the ratio of cyclical GDP to trend GDP).[5] The Hodrick and Prescott (2007) filter method was used to separate cycles from trend (and is further explained in Hingley and Park 2015b).

Filings P are transformed as indicated to $\ln(P/L)$. This allows for a standardisation between countries because L is a proxy for country size, and for stabilising the error by using the logarithmic transformation. Based on Ditka (2006), the value of R is lagged by five years in order to incorporate the concept that R&D expenditures take time to produce patentable inventions. The effects of possible booms and/or recessions within the forecast period can be assessed by manipulating u. Table 1 shows some sample statistics associated with the calculated u. The table illustrates that business cycles vary by country. Of course, there are common global shocks. But not all of these shocks are transmitted to national economies in the same way. Some economies are better insulated against external shocks, depending upon on their policy or institutional regimes. Furthermore, different countries may be in different phases of the business cycle. Hence, our decomposition method has been applied separately to each of the countries in the sample.

The model is fitted over a group of countries that includes a rest-of-the-world (ROW) class. We forecast total filings usually up to 6 years beyond the training data period. In order to obtain the forecasts for filings in a future year, the individual forecasts derived from the model by country are summed across countries. At the level of filings P, the assumed distribution of the error ε, and hence also that of P itself, is assumed to be lognormal. The technique for estimation takes this into account. Other reported studies have often not done this kind of transformation and have therefore worked with imprecise confidence intervals. Let $v = P/L$, with log (v) distributed $N(\mu, \sigma^2)$, a normal distribution with mean μ and variance σ^2. The model contains fixed effects—a separate intercept for each of 28 countries (α_{01}, α_{02}, …, α_{028})—and common slope parameters (α_1, α_2, α_3, α_4 and α_5). The linear model is fitted to the transformed data for the various countries simultaneously to determine the estimates of $\hat{\mu}$ and $\hat{\sigma}^2$ for each country. This is done in the usual way by gathering the data underlying the independent variables, including the {0, 1} dummy variables for the intercepts, into an $(n \times p)$ design matrix Z. The parameters to be estimated are themselves stacked into a $(p \times 1)$ parameter vector B. Let ^{T} indicate transposition:

[5]GDP expenditures are obtained from the World Bank's *World Development Indicators* and *Penn World Tables* https://pwt.sas.upenn.edu for Taiwan, standardised to real constant 2005 PPP international dollars.

Table 1 Sample statistics of the business cycle variable, u

Country	Mean of 'u'	Standard deviation	Coefficient of variation	Minimum	Maximum
Australia	−0.0041	1.0368	−252.0	−3.006	2.389
Austria	−0.0038	1.0803	−281.5	−2.357	2.319
Belgium	−0.0042	0.9825	−235.8	−2.076	2.229
Brazil	−0.0186	2.3141	−124.7	−5.733	6.845
Canada	−0.0091	1.3563	−149.2	−2.625	2.551
China incl. Hong Kong	0.0239	1.7829	74.6	−4.102	4.748
Denmark	−0.0087	1.3356	−153.6	−3.213	2.823
Finland	−0.0274	2.1292	−77.7	−4.936	4.864
France	−0.0049	0.9082	−187.1	−2.161	1.828
Germany	−0.0051	1.2824	−249.5	−3.634	2.369
Greece	−0.0231	1.4292	−61.9	−3.931	2.798
Ireland	−0.0239	1.7995	−75.3	−3.542	5.188
Israel	−0.0088	1.4782	−168.5	−2.747	4.436
Italy	−0.0050	1.1286	−223.8	−3.133	2.315
Japan	−0.0073	1.2073	−165.8	−3.868	2.329
Korea, Republic	−0.0025	2.0373	−802.1	−6.688	4.039
Netherlands	−0.0063	1.1360	−179.3	−1.772	2.619
New Zealand	−0.0117	1.1756	−100.4	−3.343	1.880
Norway	−0.0071	1.1159	−157.8	−2.527	2.328
Portugal	−0.0217	1.6022	−73.9	−2.746	2.933
Singapore	−0.0110	2.4053	−217.8	−5.976	5.154
Spain	−0.0140	1.0673	−76.0	−1.667	2.389
Sweden	−0.0102	1.5008	−146.9	−5.095	2.964
Switzerland	−0.0065	1.0879	−167.2	−1.695	2.693
Taiwan	0.0016	1.6706	1068.9	−5.143	3.414
United Kingdom	−0.0133	1.2229	−92.0	−2.612	2.756
United States	−0.0084	1.2254	−145.2	−3.400	1.860
World_ROW	−0.0059	1.1772	−199.4	−2.738	2.159

Notes $u = 100 \times$ (cycle/trend), where GDP = trend + cycle; i.e., using the Hodrick-Prescott filter, real GDP has been decomposed into its trend and cylical components

$$B^T = [\alpha_{01}, \alpha_{02}, \ldots, \alpha_{028}, \alpha_1, \alpha_2, \alpha_3, \alpha_4, \alpha_5]$$

$$Z = \begin{bmatrix} 1 & 0 & \ldots & 0 & a_{1,1} & a_{2,1} & a_{3,1} & a_{4,1} & a_{5,1} \\ 1 & 0 & \ldots & 0 & a_{1,2} & a_{2,2} & a_{3,2} & a_{4,2} & a_{5,2} \\ . & . & . & . & . & . & . & . & . \\ 1 & 0 & \ldots & 0 & a_{1,24} & a_{2,24} & a_{3,24} & a_{4,24} & a_{5,24} \\ 0 & 1 & \ldots & 0 & a_{1,25} & a_{2,25} & a_{3,25} & a_{4,25} & a_{5,25} \\ 0 & 1 & \ldots & 0 & a_{1,26} & a_{2,26} & a_{3,26} & a_{4,26} & a_{5,26} \\ . & . & . & . & . & . & . & . & . \\ 0 & 1 & \ldots & 0 & a_{1,48} & a_{2,48} & a_{3,48} & a_{4,48} & a_{5,48} \\ . & . & . & . & . & . & . & . & . \\ . & . & . & . & . & . & . & . & . \\ . & . & . & . & . & . & . & . & . \\ 0 & 0 & \ldots & 1 & a_{1,792} & a_{2,792} & a_{3,792} & a_{4,792} & a_{5,672} \end{bmatrix}$$

where $a_{i,j}$ is the value of the independent variable i for the jth observation in the dataset. The parameter estimates $\hat{\mathrm{B}}$ are calculated by least squares and the associated error variance of ε is calculated as $\hat{\sigma}^2$:

$$\hat{\mathrm{B}} = Z \cdot \left(Z^T Z\right)^{-1} \cdot Z^T \cdot \log(v)$$
$$\hat{\sigma}^2 = (\log(v) - Z\hat{\mathrm{B}})^T \cdot (\log(v) - Z\hat{\mathrm{B}})/(n-p)$$

where log(v) is the ($n \times 1$) vector log $(v_{1,1}, v_{1,2}, \ldots, v_{1,24}, v_{2,1}, \ldots, v_{28,672})^T$, that is the string of transformed observations (or differences in transformed observations) from each country by years in the training set, laid out with years within countries repeating faster than countries.

On the logarithmic scale, the fitted values of the observations are given by the matrix inner product $Z\hat{\mathrm{B}}$ within the training set. The forecasts for each country for each future time point are given by projecting further ($1 \times p$) rows z that are equivalent to rows of Z but taking independent variables beyond the data set and calculating the inner product $z\hat{\mathrm{B}}$.

The lognormal distribution of v has mean $\gamma = \exp(\mu + \sigma^2/2)$ and variance $\mathrm{Var}[\gamma] = \gamma^2\,(\exp(\sigma^2) - 1)$ (see Johnson et al. 1994). The fitted values on the scale of v are therefore taken from the linear model as $\hat{\gamma} = \exp((z\hat{\mathrm{B}}) + \hat{\sigma}^2/2)$. The estimated number of filings from a country at a given time point is then $w = L\hat{\gamma}$, with an estimated variance, $\mathrm{Var}[w] = L^2\,\hat{\gamma}^2(\exp(\hat{\sigma}^2) - 1)$.

It should be noted that, during the forecast period beyond the training data set, it is necessary to forecast L and also the independent variables Y^T, u and R.[6] This is usually done by straight line regression projection from the 10 most recent available years of data in the training set, and is a source of additional variability for the forecasts. The goal is to forecast Total filings as the sum of the forecasted filings per country of origin. This is $\hat{\mathrm{w}}_{\mathrm{TOTAL}} = \sum \mathrm{w} = \sum \mathrm{L}_i \hat{\gamma}_i$, where $\sum$ indicates summation over countries. $\hat{\gamma}_i$ is the filings estimate for country i.

In the following, Ξ is the (28 × 28) covariance matrix between countries on the log scale, that is estimated from the linear model by $\hat{\Xi} = \left(Z^T Z\right)^{-1} \hat{\sigma}^2$. Two alternative approaches are taken to estimate the variance of $\hat{\mathrm{w}}_{\mathrm{TOTAL}}$:

1. The sum of the estimated variances for the countries.

$$\mathrm{Var}[\hat{\mathrm{w}}_{\mathrm{TOTAL}}] = \mathrm{Var}\left[\sum_i L_i \cdot \hat{\gamma}_i\right] = \sum_i L_i^2 \cdot \hat{\gamma}_i^2 \left(\exp(\hat{\Xi}_{ii}) - 1\right)$$

   The summation is over all countries i: 1, …, 28.
2. The sum of the estimated covariances for all pairs of countries i and j.

$$\mathrm{Var}[\hat{\mathrm{w}}_{\mathrm{TOTAL}}] = \mathrm{Var}\left[\sum_i L_i \cdot \hat{\gamma}_i\right] = \sum_i L_i \sum_j L_j \cdot \hat{\gamma}_i \cdot \hat{\gamma}_j \left(\exp(\hat{\Xi}_{ij}) - 1\right)$$

   This uses a formula for the variance of a sum that is based on an extension of the formula for the variance of the mean of the lognormal distribution (Soderlind 2013). The summation is over all country pairs i and j. The country pairs include each country paired with itself, in which case the covariance term is the same as the term that feeds into expression 1 above.

Approach 1 is slightly easier to calculate than approach 2, but the covariances are likely to be relevant effects, since the model is fitted simultaneously over countries with some common parameters between countries, with international common developments affecting patent filings in many countries at the same time, and because of possible non-stationarity of the historical training set data (Ditka 2006). Approach 2 helps to take account of these factors. Here $\mathrm{Var}[\hat{\mathrm{w}}_{\mathrm{TOTAL}}]$ will be calculated by both approaches. The estimates will be compared to get an idea of stability of the model and to assess the attempts to assure stationarity by differencing both the variables.

As was already mentioned, a linear trend approach is used to forecast the independent variables Y^T, u, and R, that are then included as inputs to Z in order to use the estimated parameter matrix $\hat{\mathrm{B}}$ to find the fitted values $\hat{\gamma}_i$ for each country i for each forecasted year outside the training data set. In the case of R, the assumed

[6]Forecasts for Y^T and u are obtained from the HP filter. Since R is lagged 5 years, observed historical values can be used for the first few future forecasted years before trending is required.

5 year lag means that historical known values can be used for the forecasts of the next few years in the future. Since the model includes autoregressive terms that relate to lags of filings at one and two years, the forecasts for more than two years out themselves use inputs of filings forecasts from one and two years previously. These inputted forecasts are subject to variability by the same error process, and the other inputs are also subject to error because of the usage of a trend to estimate them. Therefore it is likely that $\mathrm{Var}[\hat{w}_{\mathrm{TOTAL}}]$, as given directly either by method 1 or 2 above, is not great enough to cover all the variability that is inherent in this approach. In order to cope with this to some extent, a pragmatic compound variance method is used. The variance of the filings forecast for a future year is taken as the sum of the variances, by either method 1 or 2, taken over all the forecasted years up to and including *s*:

$$\mathrm{Var}[(\hat{w}_{\mathrm{TOTAL}})_s] = \sum_{l=1}^{s} \mathrm{var}(\hat{w}_{\mathrm{TOTAL}})_l$$

From this variance, 95 % confidence limits for the forecast of total filings in a future year are calculated by the usual normal assumption, $(\hat{w}_{\mathrm{TOTAL}})_s \pm 1.96 * \mathrm{SE}[(\hat{w}_{\mathrm{TOTAL}})_s]$, where SE indicates standard error and is the square root of $\mathrm{Var}[(\hat{w}_{\mathrm{TOTAL}})]$. The confidence limits are appropriate for the predicted values of the mean. The mean is forecasted because the process uses essentially unchanging historical training data for all years up to the last year in the data set, with only one added data point per country in each successive annual forecasting exercise.[7]

3 Results

3.1 Model Estimates

The model is fitted to a 28 source country-of-origin data set using their annualised EPO total filings from 1990 to 2013.[8] The linear model is fitted both to the levels

[7] Alternative confidence interval/prediction interval formulae are given in the literature (Draper and Smith 1981), depending whether the intervals are sought for the mean or for an individual new observation.

[8] 27 individual countries were the following, together with a residual 28th group "ZZ" that represented the residual between the measured total filings in a year and the sum from the 27 countries, as described at European Patent Office (2015): Australia (AU), Austria (AT), Belgium (BE), Brazil (BR), Canada (CA), China & Hong Kong (CN-HK), Denmark (DK), Finland (FI), France (FR), Germany (DE), Hellas (GR), Ireland (IE), Israel (IL), Italy (IT), Japan (JP), Republic of Korea (KR), The Netherlands (NL), New Zealand (NZ), Norway (NO), Portugal (PT), Singapore (SG), Spain (ES), Sweden (SE), Switzerland (CH), Taiwan (TW), United Kingdom (GB), United States of America (US), Others (ZZ). The analysis reported here was done in mid 2014, before GDP data were updated to give results in Hingley and Park (2015a).

Table 2 Estimates of the log-linear model

Parameter		Model in levels		Model in differences	
		Estimate	Standard error	Estimate	Standard error
α_1	AR1	0.823	0.038	−0.072	0.039
α_2	AR2	0.043	0.036	−0.045	0.037
α_3	R	−0.013	0.027	−0.050	0.103
α_4	Y^T	0.444	0.075	2.145	0.395
α_5	u	0.860	0.414	1.109	0.356
Error variance		0.0228		0.0247	
Data point standard deviation		0.151		0.157	

Notes Model for EPO filings with training data set from for Levels (1990–2013) and Differences (1991–1990 to 2013–2012). Country fixed effects are included (not shown). AR1 and AR2 are one year and two year lags respectively for standardised patent filings, R is standardised R&D expenditure by business sector, Y^T is the trend level of standardised GDP, u is the business cycle variable). Also shown are Error variance and its square root, data point standard deviation. See Footnote 8 for the key to the country names

data and to the first-differences data. The parameter estimates and standard errors obtained by both approaches are shown in Table 2. Following Park (2006), the intercept α_0 is allowed to vary from country to country while the other parameters α_1 to α_5 are considered as common over countries so that pooled estimates are obtained The 5 slopes appertaining to α_1 to α_5 are shown in Table 2. The standard deviations of a data point estimate at the bottom of the table are similar for the two approaches. In terms of formal significance testing, several of the parameter estimates are not statistically different from zero under an assumption of normality, in that the absolute value of the estimate is more than 1.965 times its estimated standard error.

For the model in levels, all parameter estimates are significant by this approximate test except for the second order autoregression (AR2) and R. But for the model in differences, all the country intercepts are not significant except those for BR, CN-HK, KR, NZ, PT, SG and ES. AR1, AR2 and R are technically not significant as well, although AR1 is almost significant. However, we believe that all the included variables are useful structural descriptors of the process and should remain in the model to assist in making the forecasts. The structural dependency of the model on the parameters is manifested for the model in levels, where the non-stationary process is adequately described. What is not guaranteed for levels is the extent to which the set of independent variables is causal for the filings process.

For the model in differences, the significance is also assessed at the level of differences, and it may be that effects are in fact significant when the data are transformed back to levels. We do not succumb to the temptation to remove parameters in order to obtain a reduced model where every remaining parameter is statistically significant. There are 672 observations for the model in levels and 644 observations for the model in differences, so the removal of 33 degrees of freedom for estimation does not seriously degrade the quality of the residual sum of squares that is used to estimate the error terms.

At least for the model in differences, no particular importance should be given to the sign (positive or negative) of a parameter estimate, even when it is significant. A process by which differences of an independent variable have an effect on differences in filings, particularly after transformation, can look negative when it would in fact be positive back on the scale of levels.

Common economic factors that affect patenting in several countries at the same time, as well as the pooling of parameter estimation over the countries, induces some correlations between the parameter estimates. Table 3 shows simplified parameter correlation matrices for both levels and differences. Since the 28 intercepts behaved rather similarly to each other in terms of correlations, examples are shown only for countries from the four important sources: China, Germany, Japan and US.

Table 3 Correlation coefficients for parameter estimates

Models in levels									
Parameter	CN-HK	DE	JP	US	AR1	AR2	R	Y^T	u
CN-HK	1	0.996	0.996	0.996	0.260	0.068	0.100	−0.951	0.072
DE	0.996	1	0.999	0.999	0.254	0.066	0.085	−0.953	0.072
JP	0.996	0.999	1	0.999	0.254	0.069	0.074	−0.949	0.071
US	0.996	0.999	0.999	1	0.255	0.068	0.075	−0.949	0.072
AR1	0.260	0.254	0.254	0.255	1	−0.910	0.004	−0.224	−0.041
AR2	0.068	0.066	0.069	0.068	−0.910	1	−0.188	−0.008	0.046
R	0.100	0.085	0.074	0.075	0.004	−0.188	1	−0.376	0.067
Y^T	−0.951	−0.953	−0.949	−0.949	−0.224	−0.008	−0.376	1	0.067
u	0.072	0.072	0.071	0.072	−0.041	0.046	0.067	0.067	1
Models in differences									
Parameter	CN-HK	DE	JP	US	AR1	AR2	R	Y^T	u
CN-HK	1	0.093	0.093	0.130	−0.138	−0.137	−0.283	−0.615	0.002
DE	0.093	1	0.020	0.022	−0.035	−0.038	−0.057	−0.093	0.006
JP	0.093	0.020	1	0.025	−0.072	−0.070	−0.103	−0.075	0.001
US	0.130	0.022	0.025	1	−0.036	−0.039	−0.052	−0.152	0.005
AR1	−0.138	−0.035	−0.072	−0.036	1	0.060	0.028	−0.111	0.017
AR2	−0.137	−0.038	−0.070	−0.039	0.060	1	−0.003	−0.092	0.029
R	−0.283	−0.057	−0.103	−0.052	0.028	−0.003	1	−0.027	0.034
Y^T	−0.615	−0.093	−0.075	−0.152	−0.111	−0.092	−0.027	1	−0.047
u	0.002	0.006	0.001	0.005	0.017	0.029	0.034	−0.047	1

Notes From the model for EPO filings with the training data set in Levels and First-Differences. Country intercept correlations are shown for China, Germany, Japan and US, and are similar for the other 24 countries (See Table 2 for keys to parameter symbols)

Table 4 Total filings forecasts by the model in levels and first-differences

Year	Actual total filings	Model in levels			Model in differences		
		Total filings forecast	Standard error 1	Standard error 2	Total filings forecast	Standard error 1	Standard error 2
2013	257,457	261,929	(3105)	(3487)	263 342	(3144)	(3204)
2014		271,987	3256	3699	267,554	4520	4832
2015		287,637	4806	5510	286,476	5586	5935
2016		304,826	6184	7181	307,337	6603	7010
2017		323,868	7561	8874	331,276	6751	8094
2018		344,939	8036	10,694	358,284	7914	9232
2019		368,272	10,683	12,715	388,887	9127	10,461

Notes Standard error 1 and Standard error 2 refer to the square roots of variance methods 1 and 2 respectively for $\mathrm{Var}[\hat{w}_{\mathrm{TOTAL}}]$, as explained in Sect. 2. The results for 2013 show the model fit to the last year in the training data set, with standard errors in brackets. The cumulation of variances starts in 2015

For the model in differences, 21 out of the 36 distinct correlation coefficients have negative signs, while for the model in levels only 9 have negative signs. In general, the correlation coefficients between parameters are far less significant for the model in differences than for the model in levels. This is an indicator of stationarity for the model in differences. Looking more deeply at the model in differences, the correlations between country intercepts are positive but generally not significant, although there are relatively high correlations between CN-HK and US; and between CN-HK and KR (0.340 not shown), although not especially between KR and US (0.083 not shown). *R* has negative correlations with country intercepts, including quite a high negative value with CN-HK and with KR (−0.175 not shown). The EPO filings from CN-HK and KR have been growing more strongly over the period than from most other countries, which may have led to these effects. Rapid development of EPO patenting from CN-HK and KR may also be reasons for their significant intercepts in Table 2 in terms of the model in differences.

3.2 *Model Forecasts*

Table 4 shows the fitted values or forecasts for total filings $\hat{w}_{\mathrm{TOTAL}}$, for years 2014–2019, together with estimates of their variances $\mathrm{Var}[\hat{w}_{\mathrm{TOTAL}}]$ by the two methods. The forecasts depend on the future levels of the independent variables R, Y^T and u that are assumed.[9]

[9]For more technical details about the methodology, see Hingley and Park (2015a).

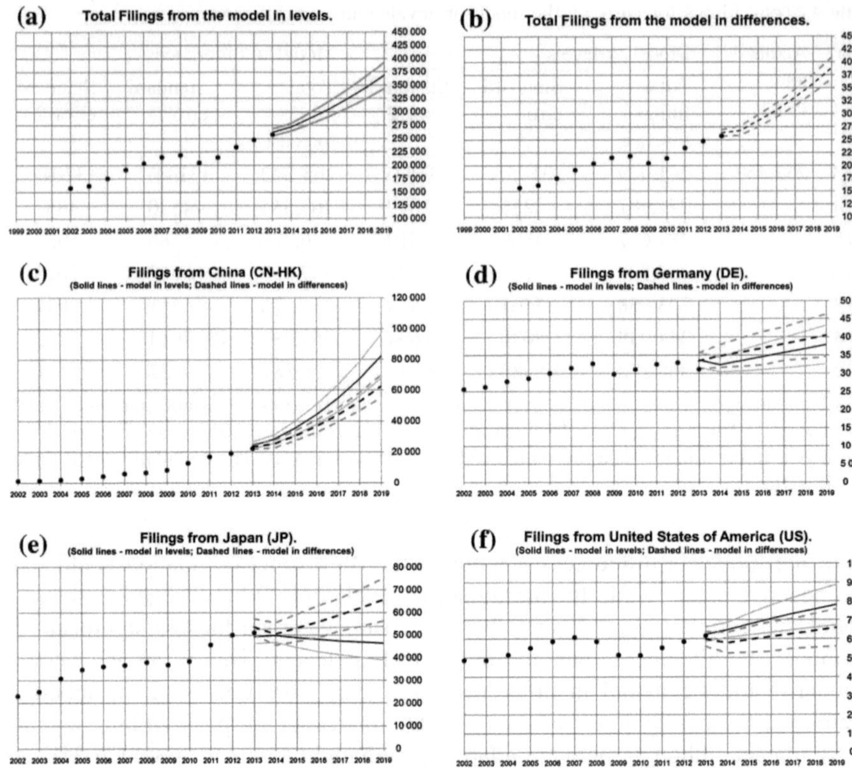

Fig. 1 Filings forecasts by the model in levels and the model in differences. *Notes Black lines* are the forecasts and grey lines are the 95 % confidence intervals for the forecasts. **a** Total filings by model in levels. **b** Total filings by model in differences. **c** Filings from China. **d** Filings from Germany. **e** Filings from Japan. **f** Filings from United States of America

Figure 1 shows a comparison between the actual and predicted values in levels and differences for the years 2014–2019. The total filings numbers are reported first, and then the filings from the important countries of origin CN-HK, DE, JP and US (as in Table 3). 95 % confidence intervals are calculated for each individual forecasted year, using the second variance method discussed in Sect. 2, and the forecasts and limits are connected over time by smoothed lines using Excel. Both models give optimistic forecasts for total filings. The model in levels proposes 368,272 in 2019, a compound annual growth rate of 6.1 % from 257,747 in 2013. The model in differences proposes 388,887 in 2019, which represents a compound annual growth rate of 7.1 % from 2013. Both models suggest low growth from 2013 to 2014 however (1.7 % for the model in levels and 3.9 % for the model in differences). Thereafter the two models roughly agree until about 2016, after which point the model in differences starts to move ahead. Forecasts towards the end of the period are of course very uncertain, so details of differences between the models out there should not be over-interpreted.

The confidence intervals widen towards the end of the forecasting period in both models. Standard error 1 is always less than standard error 2, which may indicate a tendency for positive covariances between forecasted filings for countries. At the beginning of the period, the relative sizes of the standard errors 1 and 2 are more similar for the model in differences than for the model in levels (in 2014 the ratio is 1.14 for levels and 1.07 for differences), but this situation is reversed at the end of the period (in 2019 the ratio is 1.19 for levels and 1.15 for differences). This may be related to the improved stationarity of the times series when using the model in differences.

Regarding the country forecasts in Fig. 1, there are some variations between the models for levels and differences, with levels giving higher forecasts than differences for China and United States, but differences giving higher forecasts than levels for the other two countries that are shown. For Japan (Fig. 1e), the forecasts for the model in levels decline while those in differences increase after experiencing a downward "kink" in 2014. However, this difference may not be significant because of the overlap between the confidence intervals until 2019. The strong level of projected growth for China in Fig. 1c should be noted, where about 39,000 additional filings per year are expected by 2019 compared to 2013, according to the model for differences, which makes a strong contribution to the overall increases of total filings that are envisioned in Fig. 1a, b.

4 Alternative Perspectives

This section briefly addresses some open issues, with the goal of checking for robustness and of suggesting extensions to this study. In particular, it examines three alternative ways to study the effects of business fluctuations on patenting filings at the EPO. The first is to examine quarterly data. The second is to capture cyclical movements in R&D. The third is to examine data by technological field (or sector).

Table 5 reports the results from estimating the EPO filings per-worker model on quarterly data. Column 1 shows the results for the period 1978–2011 and column 2 for a truncated period. For the quarterly data analysis, seasonal effects are controlled for by using quarterly dummies. Quarterly data are relatively noisier than annual data. Cyclical fluctuations may be small year to year, but within each year, there may be quite a bit of economic disturbances from month to month or quarter to quarter. However, what the results seem to indicate is that while patenting can vary with the business cycle, it does not vary strongly with short frequency business cycles. The 'u' variable is insignificant at explaining EPO filings.

The reason that short frequency business cycles are not a strong determinant of EPO filings is that quarter-to-quarter disturbances are relatively transient and unpredictable. It does not seem prudent for businesses to make innovation decisions based on such events. The objective of innovation is to develop new products and processes to improve efficiency or productivity, maintain or expand market share,

Table 5 Main regression model estimated using quarterly data

Sample period	(1)	(2)
	EPO filings	
	1978–2011	1978–2011
L.pl	0.400***	0.354***
	(0.023)	(0.025)
*L*2.pl	0.339***	0.339***
	(0.022)	(0.025)
yl	0.435***	0.255**
	(0.110)	(0.116)
rl	0.108***	0.195***
	(0.026)	(0.032)
u	0.149	0.140
	(0.099)	(0.104)
year	0.004**	0.005**
	(0.002)	(0.002)
1st Quarter		−9.480**
		(4.486)
2nd Quarter	0.093***	−9.392**
	(0.014)	(4.486)
3rd Quarter	−0.004	−9.487**
	(0.013)	(4.486)
4th Quarter	0.117***	-9.361**
	(0.014)	(4.485)
Country fixed effects	Included	Included
Observations	1590	1431

Dependent Variable: pl = ln(patents/worker)
Standard errors in parentheses: *$p < 0.1$, **$p < 0.05$, ***$p < 0.01$
Notes pl denotes natural log of patents per worker, *L* one-period lag, *L2* two-period lag, yl denotes real GDP per worker, rl real business enterprise R&D (BERD) per worker, 'year' denotes the time trend, and '*u*' the business cycle measure where u = cycle/trend of GDP. 1st, …, 4th quarter are dummy variables for their respective quarters

and strengthen the brand and core competencies of the firm. Innovation therefore typically targets a firm's long run profitability, which is why patenting and innovation are expected to depend, in general, on longer run factors, but as was seen with the results earlier with the annual data and discussion of the theory, year-to-year business cycles can nevertheless affect the availability of resources for innovation (or potentially the opportunity cost of innovation)—hence the sensitivity of annual patent filings to long frequency business cycles.

But at the quarterly data level, the time interval is fairly short. Firms typically seek other means to gain or maximize shorter run profits, such as financial or portfolio investments, derivatives, swaps, pricing strategies (such as discounts, non-linear pricing, price discrimination), or employment strategies (using contractors and temporary workers). Firms generally do not use R&D investments to manipulate and influence short run profits. Principally, R&D and patenting strategies are for time horizons longer than a few quarters—hence the reason why business cycles are more likely to affect patenting across years rather than across quarters.

The next issue is whether other aspects of the model also undergo cyclical shocks. In the analysis thus far, only GDP was separated into its trend and cyclical components. It may also be possible for business R&D expenditures to have a cyclical and a trend component. This was investigated, and the results are shown in Table 6. The table introduces two new variables upon applying the Hodrick-Prescott (HP) filter to R&D: trend R&D per worker and the ratio of cyclical R&D to trend R&D (uR). The uR variable is statistically insignificant at conventional levels, whether the sample period is 1978–2011 or the shorter one of 1990–2011. It is also insignificant whether we omit or control for business cycles in GDP. Thus, for now,

Table 6 Extensions: cyclicality of research and development

Sample period	(1)	(2)	(3)	(4)
	1978–2011	1990–2011	1978–2011	1990–2011
L.pl	0.685***	0.783***	0.684***	0.783***
	(0.030)	(0.040)	(0.030)	(0.040)
L2.pl	0.131***	0.043	0.132***	0.044
	(0.025)	(0.038)	(0.025)	(0.038)
ln (GDP per worker)	0.456***	0.475***		
	(0.078)	(0.089)		
ln (Trend GDP per worker)			0.444***	0.449***
			(0.079)	(0.093)
u			0.768	0.928**
			(0.597)	(0.458)
ln (Trend R&D per worker)	0.078**	0.066*	0.080**	0.071*
	(0.037)	(0.037)	(0.037)	(0.037)
uR	−0.005	0.216	−0.051	0.158
	(0.202)	(0.146)	(0.219)	(0.157)
year	0.001	0.001	0.001	0.001
	(0.002)	(0.002)	(0.002)	(0.002)
Country fixed effects	Included	Included	Included	Included
Observations	890	615	890	615

Dependent Variable: pl = ln(EPO Filings/worker)

Standard errors in parentheses: $*p < 0.1$, $**p < 0.05$, $***p < 0.01$

Notes pl denotes natural log of patents per worker, *L* one-period lag, *L2* two-period lag, *u* = cycle/trend of ratio of real GDP and uR = cycle/trend ratio of Real Business R&D per worker, year denotes the time trend

Separate intercepts for each country (or country fixed effects) were included but the estimates are not reported to conserve space

cyclical movements in R&D do not seem to affect patent filings at the EPO. This suggests that patentable innovations are a function of long run R&D programs and are not influenced by short run boosts or declines in R&D funding. But these results are for all countries and sectors pooled. It remains to be seen whether the EPO filings of individual source countries or individual sectors are more sensitive to short run movements in R&D.

A third issue is whether different technological fields are affected differently by business cycles. Table 7 offers a preliminary look using the *International Patent Classification* (IPC) sectors. According to the results shown, EPO filings in Human Necessities (IPC A), Physics (IPC G), and Electricity (IPC H) are mildly procyclical (i.e., the coefficient of '*u*' is statistically significant at the 10 % level), but filings in Chemistry (IPC C) are strongly procyclical (where the positive coefficient of '*u*' is significant at the 5 % level). For all the IPC sectors except textiles (IPC D), EPO filings are strongly influenced by trend GDP. Still, the eight IPC sectors A to H are nonetheless very broadly defined. Each of these sectors consists of diverse fields of technology. Thus, future research could study the effects of cyclical shocks at a more disaggregated IPC level.

Another related issue is whether business cycles affect the EPO filings of different source countries differently. For good country-by-country analyses, more time-series observations are needed. Tentatively, therefore, this section provides a sample of results for the U.S., a major contributor to EPO filings. As shown in Table 8, business cycles have a positive and statistically significant effect on total U.S. filings at the EPO, where by 'total' it is meant aggregate sectors (see column 1). By individual sector, U.S. EPO filings in Performing Operations and Transportation (IPC B), Mechanical Engineering, Physics, and Electricity (IPC F, G, and H) are all significantly pro-cyclical. These results are for the annual sample. The quarterly sample results are quite similar (results not shown); the only difference is that the filings in Human Necessities are also significantly pro-cyclical in the quarterly sample. For EPO applications, the business cycle variable '*u*' is only statistically significant for Electricity (IPC H), and only at the 10 % level (the results are also not shown to conserve space). With more data, a richer analysis of business cycles at the national level can and should be pursued.[10]

5 Other Applications

A side benefit of the modelling approach taken here is that the common effects over source countries for EPO filings can be analysed. Table 3 looked at correlations between countries in terms of their estimated intercept parameters. Another way is

[10]For U.S. domestic patenting, the longer time-series data of the United States Patent and Trademark Office (USPTO) could be exploited. For other countries, WIPO has very long time-series data on resident patenting. Lessons could be learned from these datasets as well.

Table 7 Extensions: business cycles by IPC sector

IPC code	Human necessities	Perform oper; transportation	Chemistry	Textiles	Fixed constructions	Mechanical	Physics	Electricity
	A	B	C	D	E	F	G	H
L.pl	0.609***	0.530***	0.621***	0.418***	0.397***	0.516***	0.667***	0.576***
	(0.032)	(0.032)	(0.033)	(0.038)	(0.035)	(0.032)	(0.033)	(0.033)
L2.pl	0.159***	0.188***	0.145***	0.239***	0.173***	0.147***	0.067**	0.146***
	(0.028)	(0.027)	(0.030)	(0.033)	(0.029)	(0.028)	(0.029)	(0.031)
yl	0.044***	0.450***	0.502***	0.406	0.543***	0.804***	0.625***	0.658***
	(0.094)	(0.097)	(0.120)	(0.269)	(0.137)	(0.123)	(0.124)	(0.134)
rl	0.018	0.088**	0.100**	0.203**	0.196***	0.062	0.152***	0.263***
	(0.042)	(0.042)	(0.050)	(0.083)	(0.052)	(0.051)	(0.048)	(0.060)
u	1.144*	0.204	1.674**	−0.325	−0.219	0.676	1.177*	1.462*
	(0.654)	(0.644)	(0.744)	(1.146)	(0.804)	(0.758)	(0.725)	(0.841)
year	0.007***	0.004*	0.000	−0.006	0.010***	0.005**	0.004*	0.004
	(0.002)	(0.002)	(0.002)	(0.004)	(0.003)	(0.002)	(0.002)	(0.003)
Country fixed effects	Included	Included	Included	Included	Included	Included	Included	Included
Observations	855	859	821	693	791	827	817	815

Dependent Variable: pl = ln(EPO Filings/worker)
Standard errors in parentheses: $*p < 0.1$, $**p < 0.05$, $***p < 0.01$
Notes pl denotes natural log of patents per worker, *L* one-period lag, *L2* two-period lag
yl denotes real GDP per worker, rl real business enterprise R&D (BERD) per worker, and *u* the business cycle measure, where *u* = cycle/trend of GDP, and year denotes the time trend
Separate intercepts for each country (or country fixed effects) were included, but the estimates are not reported to conserve space

Table 8 Extensions: EPO Filings by the U.S. and Cyclical Shocks

Sector (IPC)	Overal aggregate	Human necessities	Perform Oper; transportation	Chemistry	Textiles	Fixed constructions	Mechanical	Physics	Electricity
		A	B	C	D	E	F	G	H
	(1)	(2)	(3)	(4)	(5)	(6)	(7)	(8)	(9)
L.pl	0.759***	0.610*	0.645**	0.409	0.452	0.239	−0.001	0.667***	0.847***
	(0.193)	(0.297)	(0.252)	(0.277)	(0.344)	(0.220)	(0.149)	(0.033)	(0.214)
L2.pl	−0.424**	0.008	−0.346	0.064	−0.060	−0.063	0.069	0.067**	−0.195
	(0.197)	(0.287)	(0.248)	(0.250)	(0.251)	(0.221)	(0.144)	(0.029)	(0.220)
rl	0.314	−0.468	−0.233	2.006**	−0.208	1.783**	0.305	0.625***	0.516
	(0.389)	(0.432)	(0.491)	(0.700)	(1.128)	(0.821)	(0.341)	(0.124)	(0.704)
yl	2.512***	2.438**	3.395***	0.442	3.162	−1.313	1.154**	1.154**	1.304
	(0.764)	(0.872)	(1.141)	(0.888)	(2.779)	(1.019)	(0.480)	(0.480)	(1.350)
u	2.201**	1.404	2.267**	0.576	1.718	1.705	2.522***	3.696**	4.372***
	(0.772)	(1.042)	(0.987)	(1.063)	(2.311)	(1.543)	(0.689)	(1.424)	(1.453)
year	−0.016**	−0.011	−0.030**	−0.041***	−0.053	0.037**	0.021**	−0.011	−0.015
	(0.007)	(0.009)	(0.012)	(0.013)	(0.042)	(0.017)	(0.009)	(0.012)	(0.013)
Constant	−3.453	−5.488	15.809	56.808***	64.464	−83.157**	−67.772***	−14.548	8.204
	11.740)	(17.284)	(15.258)	(17.277)	(53.035)	(35.474)	(20.169)	(20.278)	(16.991)
Observations	22	22	22	22	22	22	22	22	22

Dependent Variable: pl = ln(EPO Filings/worker)
Standard errors in parentheses: $^{*}p < 0.1$, $^{**}p < 0.05$, $^{***}p < 0.01$
Notes pl denotes natural log of patents per worker, *L* one-period lag, *L2* two-period lag
u = cycle/trend of ratio of real GDP and uR = cycle/trend ratio of Real Business R&D per worker
year denotes the time trend

Table 9 Correlation Coefficients between countries for one-year ahead 'transformed' filings

Model in differences				
Parameter	CN-HK	DE	JP	US
CN-HK	1	0.019	−0.006	0.020
DE	0.019	1	−0.022	0.015
JP	−0.006	−0.022	1	−0.006
US	0.020	0.015	−0.006	1

Notes From the model in first-differences for EPO filings, using the training data set from 1991 to 2013. The correlation coefficients between countries are for the one-year-ahead filings estimates on the transformed scale. Inter-country correlations are shown for China, Germany, Japan and US

to determine the correlation matrix of transformed filings estimates between countries ($\hat{\Xi}$ in Sect. 2). This may indicate common behavioural patterns between applicants in groups of countries that could be associated with the overall degree of industrialisation, possession of common industries with similar patenting behaviours, geographic proximity, and so forth. Table 9 shows the derived country correlation matrix for 2013 between the major source countries for the model in differences.

The correlations between these forecasts for total filings in 2013 from the most important countries are low and can be considered to be non-significant. From the full 28 country set, pairs of countries that have the largest positive correlations are those of Ireland with Greece (0.29) and with Spain (0.21); Portugal with Singapore (0.15); and China with Denmark (0.14). Pairs of countries with negative correlations are less prominent, the largest in size being Greece with Other countries (−0.13 – 0.09). While it may be tempting to suggest causal inferences about the relationships between these countries, one should be cautious about the power of the analysis and the lack of clarity regarding possibilities for common external causes for the associations. At any rate, such interesting questions about determining communalities of patenting behaviour between countries of origin go beyond the narrow requirements of forecasting for EPO's budgetary purposes.

6 Concluding Thoughts

The usefulness of the selected type of models has been demonstrated on historical EPO total filings data, and we recommend applying the model to year-to-year differences rather than to levels. We caution that the apparent widths of the 95 % confidence limits in diagrams such as Fig. 1 are somewhat too low, especially for the later parts of the forecasted horizon. In general, the quality of the forecasts remains dependent on the assumed future levels of independent variables for GDP and R&D, the uncertainties of which are not explicitly considered in the confidence intervals.

For future research, it would be useful to further develop the model at the industry level or at the individual country level, as more observations become available. It would also be interesting to examine how business cycles in one country are transmitted internationally to affect innovation activity in another country. Specifically, the R&D and patenting of non-European countries may be affected not only by business cycles occurring in their own countries but also by fluctuations occurring in Europe. Other directions are more technically-oriented; for example, to study and incorporate the expectations formation of patent filers. EPO filings and applications may be driven by their expectations of future business cycles. In the models studied here, the contemporary value of 'u' entered the regression models. It may be the expected 'u', say u^e (the expected value of u in some future period), that affects current patenting decisions. Likewise, applicants may be affected by their forecasts of future trend GDP or future R&D budgets in designing their current innovation strategies. Modelling the expectations process is rather complex but should be worth exploring.[11] Another technical approach is to apply dynamic panel data methods, as in Hingley and Park (2015b), to account for the lagged dependent variables and country fixed effects.

Insofar as the aim of such research is to improve filings forecasts for the EPO budget, any method must take account of all the filings even where breakdowns of the data are considered separately or in parallel. Wider research into patenting behaviour can relax this requirement to some degree. The approach described here may turn out to be useful for such studies, including extensions to separate out particular patenting sectors or regions.

Finally, we believe that the way that the lognormal data were analysed here may be of some interest for wider areas of application. While the central limit theorem implies that lognormal data can indeed be described approximately in terms of normal error theory and the usual normal confidence limits, either care should be taken that the data sets are large enough for this or otherwise an approach such as the one described here should be used.

Acknowledgment and Disclaimer We thank the European Patent Office for its sponsorship. The suggestions that are made here are the opinions of the authors, who are also responsible for any errors. The specific forecasts that are shown are not the official forecasts of EPO that are provided for internal planning purposes only. We are grateful for the comments we received at the 2015 *IP5 Statistics Working Group Meeting*, Alexandria Virginia and at the 2015 *Asia Pacific Conference on Economics and Business*, Singapore.

[11]See Dannegger and Hingley (2013) for a study on the use patent applicant surveys to infer the future expectations of applicants. In these surveys, applicants indicate their plans to file patents in various offices during the current year and the next two years. Their current intentions should reveal some information about their expectations of future market conditions.

References

Dannegger F, Peter H (2013) Predictive accuracy of survey-based forecasts for numbers of filings at the European Patent Office. World Patent Inf 35:189–200

Dikta G (2006) Time series methods to forecast patent filings. In: Hingley P, Nicolas M (eds) Forecasting innovations. Springer, Heidelberg

Draper N, Smith H (1981) Applied regression analysis, 2nd edn. Wiley, New York

European Patent Office (2015) Patent Filings Survey 2013: intentions of applicants regarding patent applications at the European Patent Office and other offices, 2014. http://www.epo.org/service-support/contact-us/surveys/future-filings.html

Hidalgo A, Gabaly S (2012) Use of prediction methods for patent and trademark applications in Spain. World Patent Inf 34(1):19–35

Hingley P, Nicolas M (2004) Methods for forecasting numbers of patent applications at the European Patent Office. World Patent Inf 26(3):191–204

Hingley P, Nicolas M (2006) Improving forecasting methods at the European Patent Office. In: Hingley P, Nicolas M (eds) Forecasting innovations. Springer, Heidelberg

Hingley P, Park W (2015a) A dynamic log-linear regression to forecast numbers of future filings at the European Patent Office. World Patent Inf 42(3):19–27

Hingley P, Park W (2015b) Do business cycles affect patenting? Evidence from European patent filings, Working Paper

Hodrick R, Prescott E (2007) Postwar business cycles: an empirical investigation. J Money Credit Banking 29:1–16

Johnson N, Kotz S, Balakrishnan N (1994) Continuous univariate distributions, vol 1. Wiley, New York

Meade N (2006) An assessment of the comparative accuracy of time series forecasts of patent filings: the benefits of disaggregation in space and time. In: Hingley P, Nicolas M (eds) Forecasting innovations. Springer, Heidelberg

Organisation for Economic Cooperation and Development (2014) Main science and technology indicators. http://www.oecd.org/sti/msti.htm

Park W (2006) International patenting at the European Patent Office: aggregate, sectoral and family filings. In: Hingley P, Nicolas M (eds) Forecasting innovations. Springer, Heidelberg

Soderlind P (2013) Lecture notes-econometrics: some statistics. http://home.datacomm.ch/paulsoderlind/Courses/OldCourses/EcmXSta.pdf

Cognitive and Affective Experience in Online Shopping: Findings from Pure-Click Customers in Indonesia

Evi Rinawati Simanjuntak and Caroline Herlina

Abstract As the number of new entrants in the e-retailing industry in Indonesia increases steeply, sustaining competitiveness becomes more challenging, especially in the pure-click business model. This research aims to establish a deeper understanding of how cognitive experiential state (CES) and affective experiential state (AES) may impact repurchase intention and to examine the role of satisfaction and trust in pure-click customers in Indonesia. A quantitative approach using a survey with convenience sampling was used as the data collection method. This study took 150 usable responses for further analysis. Structural equation modeling using LISREL 8.8 was used for hypothesis testing. The results indicated that AES affects CES directly; CES forms trust through satisfaction. On the other hand, the findings show that although AES can directly affect consumers' trust, there is no support for the direct impact of AES toward satisfaction. Meanwhile, repurchase intention is established only when trust existed.

Keywords Affective experiential state · Cognitive experiential state · e-Retailing · Online customer experience

1 Introduction

In today's highly competitive online market, creating a meaningful differential shopping experience is very important to enhance basic offerings. In the online shopping context, one of the ways to create differentiation is through online customer experience (OCE). OCE is shaped by customers' engagement with the website's cognitive and affective elements that form an impression in memory and are summed up to be the overall take-away impression (Rose et al. 2011).

E.R. Simanjuntak (✉) · C. Herlina
Bina Nusantara University, Jakarta, Indonesia
e-mail: esimanjuntak@binus.edu

C. Herlina
e-mail: caroline.herlina@yahoo.com

S. Soh (ed.), *Selected Papers from the Asia Conference on Economics & Business Research 2015*, DOI 10.1007/978-981-10-0986-0_7

2 Literature Review

Aligning the concept of co-creation of values in Service-Dominant Logic, e-Retailers are competing through service excellence (Lusch et al. 2007) that requires them to involve the interaction of organization and exchange partners in the co-creation of value. To that extent, it is possible for customers and companies to collaborate in co-creating positive online customer experience (cognitively as well as affectively) (Kohler et al. 2011).

Cognitive experiential is indicated when the purpose of processing information is to solve problems or to learn. Cognitive experiential state (CES) is described as an element of OCE that is related with the conscious thought process (Rose et al. 2012). CES works in the concept of '*flow*' in which the person is fully captivated in doing a particular activity until becoming psychologically absorbed and inattentive to time and circumstances surrounding them (Csikszentmihalyi 1997).

Affective experiential state (AES) is an element of OCE that generates moods, feelings, and emotions. Emotional feeling is an important element in shaping cognitive processes, since it influences the fetching and understanding of information from memory (Bower 1981). It was also argued that both cognitive and affective experience elements are involved in the formation of customer satisfaction (Homburg et al. 2006). These arguments lead to the following hypotheses:

H1: Affective experiential state will positively influence the cognitive experiential state.

H2: Cognitive experiential state will positively impact on online shopping satisfaction.

H3: Affective experiential state will positively impact on online shopping satisfaction.

Cognitive elements can influence initial trust formation by means of cognitive assessment on an e-Retailer's reputation (Eastlick and Lotz 2011). Site quality that induces affective experience was found to affect the forming of initial trust (Koufaris and Hampton-Sosa 2004). Referring to the above arguments, the following hypotheses are constructed:

H4: Cognitive experiential state will positively impact on the formation of trust in online shopping.

H5: Affective experiential state will positively impact on the formation of trust in online shopping.

In the e-retailing context, studies also prove the positive implication of satisfaction on trust (Pavlou 2003). Therefore, the following hypothesis is derived:

H6: Online shopping satisfaction will positively impact on the formation of trust in online shopping.

Satisfaction affects loyalty and intention to repurchase (Lim et al. 2014). As a behavioral belief, trust affects the willingness to make an online transaction (Amoroso and Mukahi 2013). Formally stated, the hypotheses are as follows:

Fig. 1 Conceptual model

H7: Online shopping satisfaction will positively impact on repurchase intention.
H8: Trust in online shopping will positively impact on repurchase intention.

We tested the above eight hypotheses using the framework of Rose et al. (2012) depicted in Fig. 1.

3 Methods

3.1 Sample and Data Collection

The unit of analysis in this study was individuals who have prior experience in purchasing goods or services in pure-click retailers in Indonesia. The questionnaire was distributed using a convenience sampling method, resulting in 150 usable questionnaires.

3.2 Measures of Constructs

CES was measured by the 'flow' state condition by Novak et al. (2000). AES was measured by eight semantic differential items, following Havlena and Holbrook (1986). Trust in online shopping was measured by eight items according to Lee and Turban (2001), while satisfaction and repurchase intention were measured by four items for each construct, adapting Khalifa and Liu (2007).

To ensure reliability and validity of the constructs, Confirmatory Factor Analysis (CFA) was conducted. Measurement items that show factor loading less than 0.5 will be trimmed. The CFA result shows standardized item loadings ranged from 0.62 to 0.83 and therefore displayed sufficient item validity. The constructs exhibit sufficient reliability with all composite reliability values (CR) ranging from 0.75 to 0.84 and Average Variance Extracted (AVE) ranging from 0.5 to 0.58; all met or exceeded the recommended cut-off criteria, referring to CR ≥ 0.7 and AVE ≥ 0.5.

4 Findings

4.1 Respondent Profiles

Forty seven percent of the sample is male and 53 % is female. Most of the respondents (73 %) are 21–25 years old. Respondents purchased various type of merchandise, with apparel products top of the list (43 %), followed by electronics (23 %).

4.2 Conceptual Model Testing

To test the conceptual model, we employed structural equation modeling with robust maximum likelihood estimation. Table 1 provides summary results for the tested model.

The overall fit of the structural model is significant ($\chi 2$ (124) = 181, $p < 0.01$), additional goodness-of-fit indices (IFI = 0.98, CFI = 0.98, RMSEA = 0.056) all meet or exceed the recommended cut-off criteria, referring to $\chi^2/\text{df} \leq 3$, RMSEA ≤ 0.080, CFI > 0.90, IFI > 0.90, which indicated a good fit.

Findings suggest that the affective component (AES) is crucial due to the capability to influence the cognitive component (CES). AES also shows a direct effect on trust; however, CES does not exhibit an impact to trigger trust.

The mediating role of satisfaction toward repurchase intention is not evident. However, this research finds a strong mediating effect of satisfaction in the linkage of CES to trust, suggesting that the cognitive aspect can only form trust, when satisfaction is evident. Trust mediates the linkage to repurchase intention, suggesting that only when customers have sufficient trust on the pure-click retailers, they will make another purchase.

Table 1 Estimation result on the conceptual model (N = 150)

Hypothesis sign	Path from → to	Standardized estimate	t-value	Conclusion
H1: +	AffES → CogES	0.76	9.10	Supported
H2: +	CogES → Satis	0.29	1.96	Supported
H3: +	AffES → Satis	−0.03	*−0.18*	*Not supported*
H4: +	CogES → Trust	0.01	*0.05*	*Not supported*
H5: +	AffES → Trust	0.28	2.00	Supported
H6: +	Satis → Trust	0.65	6.16	Supported
H7: +	Satis → RepInt	−0.04	*−0.49*	*Not supported*
H8: +	Trust → RepInt	0.87	5.38	Supported

5 Contribution, Managerial Implication, Limitations, and Further Research

This research contributes to the OCE research by analyzing separately the impact of each dimensions of OCE (i.e., CES and AES) in forming repurchase intention. Another contribution is made by extending OCE in the context of pure-click retailers in a developing country. The impact is tested on online retailers across sectors rather than focusing on a specific industry.

This study advises online retailers to focus on AES (i.e., a more organized, easy-to-follow website). Providing personalized website displays according to a customer's profile is presumed to increase affective experience that can induce purchase intention. This study also identifies further implication on trust handling in pure-click retailers; a high level of AES and CES will be meaningless if trust is under-managed. Pure-click retailers need to mitigate this by providing external validation to their security in the transaction system.

This research is constrained by several limitations. First, this study does not differentiate online experience types (e.g., search, purchase, consumption, and after-sale experiences), hence may impact the evaluation of an e-Retailer. Future research could accommodate these elements to the model. Second, this study does not look at other elements that might affect a customer's overall experience while shopping online (e.g., personal and uncontrollable factors—cultural, sociological, etc.); future studies can accommodate these factors. Third, the study is done in the context of a developing country, in which the technological infrastructure could be different from developed countries; therefore, generalization of the conclusion should be done with caution.

References

Amoroso DL, Mukahi T (2013) An examination of consumers' high and low trust as constructs for predicting online shopping behavior. J Electron Commer Organ 11(1):1–17

Bower GH (1981) Mood and memory. Am Psychol 36(2):129–148

Csikszentmihalyi M (1997) Finding flow: the psychology of engagement with everyday life. Basic Books

Eastlick MA, Lotz S (2011) Cognitive and institutional predictors of initial trust toward an online retailer. Int J Retail Distrib Manag 39(4):234–255

Havlena WJ, Holbrook MB (1986) The varieties of consumption experience: comparing two typologies of emotion in consumer behavior. J Consum Res 13(3):394–404

Homburg C, Koschate N, Hoyer WD (2006) The role of cognition and affect in the formation of customer satisfaction: a dynamic perspective. J Mark 70(3):21–31

Khalifa M, Liu V (2007) Online consumer retention: contingent effects of online shopping habit and online shopping experience. Eur J Inf Syst 16(6):780–792

Kohler T, Fueller J, Matzler K, Stieger D (2011) Co-creation of virtual worlds: the design of user experience. MIS Q 35(3):773–88

Koufaris M, Hampton-Sosa W (2004) The development of initial trust in an online company by new customers. Inf Manag 41(3):377–397

Lee MK, Turban E (2001) A trust model for consumer internet shopping. Int J Electron Commer 6(1):75–91
Lim YJ, Osman AB, Halim MSBA (2014) Perceived usefulness and trust towards consumer behaviors: a perspective of consumer online shopping. J Asian Sci Res 4(10):541–546
Lusch RF, Vargo SL, O'Brien M (2007) Competing through service: insights from service-dominant logic. J Retail 83(1):5–18
Novak TP, Hoffman DL, Yung Y-F (2000) Measuring the customer experience in online environments: a structural modeling approach. Mark Sci 19(1):22–42
Pavlou PA (2003) Consumer acceptance of electronic commerce: integrating trust and risk with the technology acceptance model. Int J Electron Commer 7(3):101–134
Rose S, Hair N, Clark M (2011) Online customer experience: a review of the business-to-consumer online purchase context. Int J Manag Rev 13(1):24–39
Rose S, Clark M, Philip S, Hair N (2012) Online customer experience in e-retailing: an empirical model of antecedents and outcomes. J Retail 88(2):308–322

Discussion of Factors Affecting Taiwan Small and Medium Enterprises' Establishment of Marketing Channels in China

Chung-Chih Lee

Abstract Ever since cross-strait direct transportation link in 2008 as well as the signing of ECFA between Taiwan and China, Taiwan has encountered new opportunities to sell fresh agricultural products to China. High economic benefit agricultural and aquatic products including grouper, tea leave and Oncidium are entitled to zero-duty niche within three years. According to statistics from the Council of Agriculture, growth momentum for Taiwan agricultural products in recent years mainly comes from mainland China. The amount of Taiwan fruits exported to China in 2009 has increased by more than 2 times compared with the one for 2008, while amount for fresh vegetable exported increased by more than 8 times. The value of Taiwan agricultural products exported in the first half of 2010 was US$1.874 billion, a 19.3 % increase compared with the one for same period of the previous year. Among them, export to China was US$23.2 billion, a 36.4 % increase compared with the one for same period of the previous year. Opinion poll conducted by Global Views Monthly indicates that over 70 % of people living in the 5 major cities of Taiwan consider that "a mayor should put agricultural product export assistance on his/her priority list." It is therefore obvious that agricultural product export which comes with substantial benefits are highly concerned by both Taiwan and China. This research focused on companies willing to explore agricultural product marketing channels in China and developed questionnaires based on the Theory of Planned Behavior ("TPB") for investigation over company management and responsible persons under the purpose of analyzing which factors will affect company management and responsible persons' willingness to explore marketing channels in China. The result indicates that company management and responsible persons' attitude, perception, and behavioral control over establishment of marketing channels in China have significant influence over their willingness to do so. It is therefore obvious that people interviewed hope that government can provide a centralized service window for companies establishing marketing channels in China in order to solve various issues involved. Furthermore, people

C.-C. Lee (✉)
The Graduate School of Business and Operations Management, Chang Jung Christian University, Tainan City 71101, Taiwan
e-mail: ltu0283691588@gmail.com; buddhalovefelix@gmail.com

S. Soh (ed.), *Selected Papers from the Asia Conference on Economics & Business Research 2015*, DOI 10.1007/978-981-10-0986-0_8

interviewed are very concerned if they understand counterparty's related laws and regulations, if they understand local consumer's needs and if they can control local existing marketing channels before their setting up of marketing channels in China. This research focuses on these issues and presents recommendations accordingly.

Keywords Agricultural products · Marketing channel · Theory of planned behavior

1 Introduction

In the face of the challenges posed by globalization, the Taiwanese Government constantly promulgates new economic policies with the goal of improving cross-strait relations and encouraging Taiwanese entrepreneurs to enter the Chinese market. Agricultural products labeled as MIT (made in Taiwan) can generate differentiation and satisfy the demand of Chinese consumers for quality assurance in the field of agricultural and fishery products. Promotion via multiple channels also contributes to the preference for high-quality agricultural products from Taiwan by Chinese consumers. Since the conclusion of the Economic Cooperation Framework Agreement (ECFA) between China and Taiwan on June 29, 2011, a total of 18 different agricultural and fishery products have been included on the "early harvest list." This benefit of preferential tariffs for these products once zero customs is enacted greatly enhances the competitiveness of agricultural and fishery products from Taiwan on the Chinese market.

Furthermore, there have been closer exchanges, interactions, and dealings between Chinese and Taiwanese farmers in recent years and a large number of Chinese officials and entrepreneurs have visited Taiwan to observe agricultural production technologies and business models of farmers' associations and recreational agriculture. At the same time, China has attracted large-scale Taiwanese investments in sophisticated agriculture. According to official Chinese statistics, Experimental Zones of Cross-Strait Agricultural Cooperation and Taiwan Farmers' Incubators have been established in 16 Chinese provinces (districts/municipalities) as of the end of 2009. Experimental zones of Cross-Strait Agricultural Cooperation were created in 9 Chinese provinces (districts/municipalities), while a total of 20 Taiwan Farmers' Incubators were set up in 12 Chinese provinces (districts/municipalities).

Statistics released by the Taiwanese Council of Agriculture reveal that export sales of Taiwanese fruit and fresh vegetables to China grew by over 200 and 800 % in 2009, respectively, compared to 2008. In the first half of 2010, the total production value of export sales of Taiwanese agricultural products amounted to 1.874 billion USD, which represents an increase by 19.3 % compared to the same period of the previous year. Exports to Mainland China reached 23.2 billion USD, which marks an increase by 36.4 % over the same period of the preceding year. Global Views Monthly conducted an opinion poll of residents of the five municipalities

(Taipei, New Taipei, Taichung, Tainan, and Kaohsiung). One of the questions asked was: "Which items should be given priority in interactions of your city with Mainland China initiated by your mayor within his term of office?" Over 70 % of all respondents think that promotion of export sales of agricultural products should be given preference. This clearly shows that export sale of agricultural products with high profit potential is an issue of high concern to Taiwanese citizens (Council of Agriculture 2015).

The Council of Agriculture states that the inauguration of direct cross-strait transportation links in 2008 has created new opportunities for the promotion of fresh agricultural produce from Taiwan in China. Upon the signing of the cross-strait ECFA agreement, agricultural products with high economic returns that are eligible for custom tariff exemption within three years include grouper, tea leaves, and dancing-lady orchids. In addition, statistics published by the Department of International Affairs of the Council of Agriculture indicate that the total export value of Taiwanese agricultural products to China amounted to only 84,600 USD in 2009. This figure immediately rose to 47.53 million USD in 2010, which represents an increase by 60 %. The grouper is a perfect example. The opening of direct cross-strait transportation links has led to frequent cross-strait shipping, allowing Chinese consumers to enjoy Taiwanese seafood and thereby stimulating the Taiwanese agriculture and fishery industry.

Due to the huge consumption potential of the Chinese market and the fact that most Chinese consumers are curious and convinced of the higher quality of Taiwanese agriculture and fishery products, the competitiveness of such products on the Chinese market has been greatly enhanced. This has also resulted in continued investments of an increasing number of farmers, farming organizations, and produce marketing firms in this market. The Council of Agriculture has however alerted these groups and organizations that the Mainland Chinese market is still an emerging market for Taiwanese businesses. Smooth customs clearance is of great importance for the export of fresh agricultural products. Businesses need a clear understanding of import procedures and legal provisions related to clearance procedures, and relevant quarantine regulations as well as local customs and habits, sales channels, and marketing conditions in China before they decide whether or not to invest in the Chinese market.

This study aims to explore the intention of Taiwanese SMEs and agriculture and fishery businesses to establish sales channels and marketing bases in China upon the signing of the ECFA agreement. It also analyzes which issues these businesses take into consideration prior to their decisions. These are the key aspects that the Council of Agriculture and businesses interested in expanding into the Chinese market must be fully aware of. The author employs the theory of planned behavior proposed by Ajzen (1991) to analyze the main factors affecting businesses that intend to establish sales channels and marketing bases in China as well as their main considerations as a reference for global product deployment and the inauguration of a new age of agriculture after the signing of ECFA.

2 Theoretical Basis

2.1 Theory of Planned Behavior

Ajzen (1988, 1991) proposed the theory of planned behavior (TPB) in 1988. This theory has been widely applied in the field of social psychology. TPB is frequently employed to analyze psychology and behavior. For instance, Shen and Qiu (2014) utilized TPB to expound the factors affecting the willingness of university faculty and staff members to adopt eco-friendly behavior patterns, while Ceren et al. (2011) employed the theory to explore the recycling behavior of 232 teachers in America. Wu (2011) examines the factors affecting the decision of farmers to adopt organic farming methods with TPB as the main research framework. Chu and Chiu (2003), on the other hand, utilize TPB to explore waste recycling behavior of families. Due to the wide application field of the theory of planned behavior, Armitage and Conner (2001) employed meta-analysis to identify and analyze 185 TPB-related research articles. They found that TPB can explain 27 % of the behavioral variance and 39 % of the behavior intention variance. This clearly indicates that TPB is a suitable tool for the analysis or explanation of human psychology and behavior.

Ajzen believes that humans adopt a certain type of behavior based on a conscious plan. Behavior intention is an indicator for the measurement of the conscious willingness of an individual to engage in a certain type of behavior or action and may also serve as a predictor of individual behavior. Based on his past research, Ajzen discovered that behavior intention is highly correlated with behavior and that it is almost identical to behavior.

The main hypothesis of TPB is as follows: The more positive the attitude of an individual toward a certain type of behavior or action, the higher the perceived support from key opinion groups, and the more control or resources the individual believes he/she has when engaging in said behavior or action, the higher is his/her intention to adopt said behavior or action. Attitude, subjective norms, and perceived behavior control therefore affect behavior intention.

As far as the respondents of this study are concerned, behavior intentions can be observed by analyzing the willingness of enterprises to establish marketing channels in China. Behavior intentions are in turn affected by attitude, subjective norms, and behavior control. The following questions are of crucial importance: 1. Do businesses believe that the establishment of marketing channels in China will give them a competitive advantage? 2. Do family members and employees of said businesses endorse and encourage the establishment of marketing channels in China? 3. What is the subjective perception of the difficulty and feasibility of the establishment of marketing channels in China on the part of businesses? In addition to the basic hypotheses stated above, Ajzen also argues that individuals determine the difficulty of engaging in a certain type of behavior or action based on past experiences and current resources and conditions. Perceived behavior control therefore indirectly affects behavior (this effect is independent of intention). As a

Fig. 1 Research framework

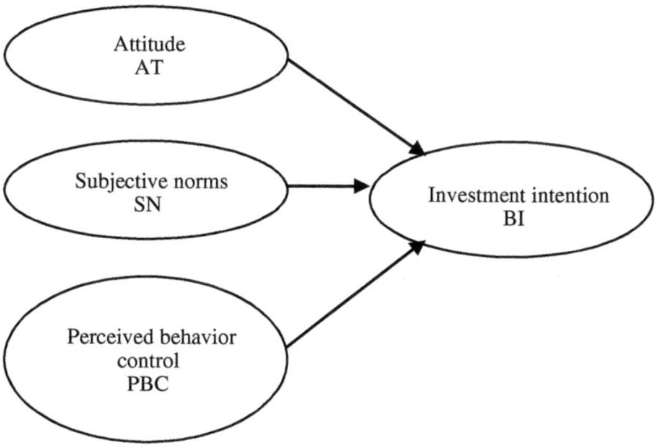

consequence, the correlation between behavior and PBC is often expressed with a broken line in the TPB model (Ajzen 1988, 1991) (Fig. 1).

All scholars including Ajzen believe that attitude is an important variable for the prediction of behavior. Lai et al. (2013), for instance, found that attitude toward behavior is positively correlated with the intention to visit a museum, while Yu-Wen Wang et al. (2013) discovered that attitude is positively correlated with the intention of teenagers to give up smoking. Wu (2011) argues that the attitude of farmers toward organic agriculture has a significant impact on the willingness to adopt organic farming methods. Hwang et al. (2000) found that attitude toward behavior has a strong impact on the intention of engaging in eco-friendly behavior, while Hines et al. (1986) discovered that a positive correlation exists between attitude toward behavior and eco-friendly behavior.

Subjective norms can be further divided into information influence and normative influence. Information influence refers to the decision of an individual to believe a certain piece of information due to its reliability, trustworthiness, and reference value (information influence dimension). On the other hand, if an individual chooses to believe a certain piece of information due to opinions, appraisals, perceptions, and reactions of key opinion groups (usually close friends), the influence is of a normative type. Ajzen and Madden (1986) pointed out in their research that perceived behavior control affects behavior in two different ways:

1. Behavior intention is a medium between perceived behavior control and behavior.
2. Perceived behavior control has a direct or indirect impact on behavior.

3 Research Method

3.1 Research Framework

Based on TPB theory, this study utilizes the following research framework and the following operational definitions of the questionnaire variables:

(a) Attitude: This study adopts the broader definition of attitude developed by Ajzen (1988, 1991), Hartmann and Apaolaza-Ibanez (2008). Cognition, emotions, even knowledge and values are included in this broader definition of attitude. Attitude-related questionnaire items designed for this research focus on expectations of businesses with regard to the Chinese market and consumers and opinions on the competitive advantage of MIT agricultural and fishery products.
(b) Subjective norms: Opinions on the Chinese market of key opinion groups including the government, chamber of commerce, employees, and family members have a potential impact on the decision of businesses to establish marketing channels in China. Respondents (businesses) were asked whether they are affected by these key opinion groups and whether or not said groups support the decision of said businesses to create new marketing channels in China. Sample statements/questions: "I am convinced that the government will provide us with support and advice" and "Does support provided by the government affect my decision to enter the Chinese market?".
(c) Perceived behavior control: Does the understanding of the Chinese market, channels, laws, and consumers play an important role in the establishment of marketing channels in China by Taiwanese businesses? It is not difficult to search for sales channels and marketing bases in China or gain a deeper understanding of the laws and regulations governing company establishment.
(d) Investment intention: Respondents were asked about their willingness to establish marketing channels in China. In view of the fact that a large number of respondents lack real experience in investment in the Chinese market, this study divides investment intention into the following three subitems: Use of existing channels in China, investments of Chinese companies in newly established companies in China, and direct establishment of new sales channels and marketing bases in China. The goal of this question design is to determine the preferences of Taiwanese businesses with regard to these three investment methods in the context of investment intentions.

3.2 Respondents and Data Collection Method

The respondent sample was obtained by distributing questionnaires during an ECFA information meeting organized by the Council of Agriculture of the Executive Yuan in Kaohsiung City. The author of this study began by asking respondents whether they were a small- or medium-sized enterprise, whether or not they were willing to establish marketing channels in China, and whether or not they specialized in the sale of agricultural and fishery products. Only respondents who met all three criteria were included in the sample. Questionnaires were distributed between March 8 and 9, 2015. A total of 192 valid questionnaires were returned.

3.3 Questionnaire Structure and Items

This study mainly relied on the definitions and question design developed by Fishbein (1980), Ajzen (1991), Armitage and Conner (2001), Chu and Chiu (2003), Lin and Yang (2005), Li et al. (2005), Wu (2011), Ceren et al. (2011), Tu et al. (2011), Wang et al. (2013), and Shen and Qiu (2014) for the identification of factors that have a potential impact on the decision of businesses to establish marketing channels in China and the development of questionnaire items for the four dimensions of attitude, subjective norms, perceived behavior control, and investment intention. A five-point Likert scale has been adopted for measurement purposes (5 = strongly agree, 4 = agree, 3 = neutral, 2 = disagree, 1 = strongly disagree).

In addition, basic background information about respondents was obtained through questions about total capital, employee numbers, business categories (commerce and service industry, fishery industry), and public listing on TWSE and TPEx (Table 1).

Table 1 Questionnaire structure and questionnaire items

Variable	Questionnaire items	Reference source
Attitude	The establishment of sales and marketing bases for agricultural and fishery products in China is a general trend	Fishbein (1980), Ajzen (1991), Wu (2011)
	China is the largest market in the vicinity of Taiwan	
	Taiwanese entrepreneurs enjoy an advantage when making investments in China due to the same language and ethnicity	
	The geographic proximity between China and Taiwan is a major incentive	
	Chinese consumers favor agricultural and fishery products from Taiwan	
	Preferential terms for Taiwanese businesses granted by the Chinese authorities will attract more investments	
	MIT products have a competitive advantage in the Chinese market	
	I can gain a rapid understanding of the attitudes and habits of Chinese consumers	
	Due to the large number of success stories, I am not worried about making an investment in China	
	An investment in China represents a great opportunity	

(continued)

Table 1 (continued)

Variable	Questionnaire items	Reference source
Subjective norms	I think the government will provide us with support and advice	Fishbein (1980), Ajzen (1991), Wu (2011)
	I think the chamber of commerce will provide us with support and advice	
	I think our employees will fully support the decision to develop marketing channels in China	
	I think my family will fully support the decision to develop marketing channels in China	
	The provision of support by the government will affect my decision to expand into the Chinese market	
	The provision of support by the chamber of commerce will affect my decision to expand into the Chinese market	
	The support from our employees will affect my decision to expand into the Chinese market	
	The support from my family will affect my decision to expand into the Chinese market	
Perceived behavior control	It is not difficult to search for sales channels and marketing bases for agricultural and fishery products in China	Fishbein (1980), Ajzen (1991), Wu (2011)
	It is not difficult to apply for capital loans from Chinese banks	
	It is not difficult to recruit new employees in China	
	It is not difficult to gain a deeper understanding of the laws and regulations governing company establishment in China	
	It is not difficult to find relevant persons in the Chinese market	
	I can quickly locate supporting industries for sales channels and marketing bases in China	
	I can quickly establish a good reputation for Taiwanese agricultural and fishery products in China	
	I can overcome the problem of preservation of fresh agricultural and fishery products during shipping	
	I can provide processed agricultural and fishery products favored by the Chinese market	
	The image and packaging of our agricultural and fishery products are favored by Chinese consumers	
Investment intention	I intend to use existing sales channels in China	Fishbein (1980), Ajzen (1991), Wu (2011)
	I intend to allow investments by Chinese companies in my newly established company	
	I intend to directly establish new sales channels and marketing bases in China	

4 Results

4.1 Opinions of Taiwanese Entrepreneurs on the Establishment of Marketing Channels in China

The results of the descriptive statistics reveal that the respondents strongly agree with the following three statements as far as attitudes toward the establishment of marketing channels are concerned: 6. Preferential terms for Taiwanese businesses granted by the Chinese authorities will attract more investments. (M = 4.21, SD = 0.50) 3. Taiwanese entrepreneurs enjoy an advantage when making investments in China due to the same language and ethnicity. (M = 4.11, SD = 0.39) 4. The geographic proximity between China and Taiwan is a major incentive. (M = 4.05, SD = 0.52).

As for subjective norms, the respondents concur with the following statements: 2. I think the chamber of commerce will provide us with support and advice. (M = 3.89, SD = 0.52) 3. I think our employees will fully support the decision to develop marketing channels in China. (M = 3.82, SD = 0.32), 8. The support from my family will affect my decision to expand into the Chinese market. (M = 3.69, SD = 0.42).

In the dimension of perceived behavior control, respondents agreed with the following statements: 3. It is not difficult to recruit new employees in China. (M = 3.92, SD = 0.51), 8. I can overcome the problem of preservation of fresh agricultural and fishery products during shipping. (M = 3.0.91, SD = 0.52), 9. I can provide processed agricultural and fishery products favored by the Chinese market (M = 3.87, SD = 0.41). It should be pointed out that mean values of less than 3 for a total of five statements indicate that respondents disagree with said statements. This shows that the respondents believe they may encounter the following problems when establishing marketing channels in China: difficulties in the search for sales channels and marketing bases for agricultural and fishery products and application for capital loans from Chinese banks, lack of knowledge about Chinese laws and regulations and relevant persons in the Chinese market as well as difficulties in the location of supporting industries for sales channels and marketing bases in China.

As far as the three investment methods in the context of investment intentions are concerned, respondents favor the direct establishment of sales channels and marketing bases in China (M = 4.12, SD = 0.23), followed by temporary use of existing sales channels in China (M = 3.98, SD = 0.34), and investments by Chinese businesses in companies established by Taiwanese entrepreneurs in China (M = 2.87, SD = 0.42). The author speculates that this phenomenon may be explained by the fact that Taiwanese entrepreneurs are still not familiar with the Chinese market and are still wary of investments by Chinese businesses (Table 2).

Table 2 Summary of descriptive statistics for opinions of Taiwanese entrepreneurs on the establishment of marketing channels in China

Variable	Questionnaire items	Mean	Standard deviation	Reliability
Attitude	The establishment of sales and marketing bases for agricultural and fishery products in China is a general trend	4.02	0.46	0.872
	China is the largest market in the vicinity of Taiwan	4.03	0.52	
	Taiwanese entrepreneurs enjoy an advantage when making investments in China due to the same language and ethnicity	4.11	0.39	
	The geographic proximity between China and Taiwan is a major incentive	4.05	0.52	
	Chinese consumers favor agricultural and fishery products from Taiwan	3.98	0.41	
	Preferential terms for Taiwanese businesses granted by the Chinese authorities will attract more investments	4.21	0.50	
	MIT products have a competitive advantage in the Chinese market	3.89	0.52	
	I can gain a rapid understanding of the attitudes and habits of Chinese consumers	3.76	0.42	
	Due to the large number of success stories, I'm not worried about making an investment in China	3.62	0.39	
	An investment in China represents a great opportunity	3.82	0.42	
Subjective norms	I think the government will provide us with support and advice	3.12	0.31	0.723
	I think the chamber of commerce will provide us with support and advice	3.89	0.52	
	I think our employees will fully support the decision to develop marketing channels in China	3.82	0.32	
	I think my family will fully support the decision to develop marketing channels in China	3.42	0.29	
	The provision of support by the government will affect my decision to expand into the Chinese market	3.03	0.32	
	The provision of support by the chamber of commerce will affect my decision to expand into the Chinese market	3.12	0.29	
	The support from our employees will affect my decision to expand into the Chinese market	3.67	0.62	
	The support from my family will affect my decision to expand into the Chinese market	3.69	0.42	

(continued)

Table 2 (continued)

Variable	Questionnaire items	Mean	Standard deviation	Reliability
Perceived behavior control	It is not difficult to search for sales channels and marketing bases for agricultural and fishery products in China	2.82	0.41	0.845
	It is not difficult to apply for capital loans from Chinese banks	2.56	0.34	
	It is not difficult to recruit new employees in China	3.92	0.51	
	It is not difficult to gain a deeper understanding of the laws and regulations governing company establishment in China	2.62	0.38	
	It is not difficult to find relevant persons in the Chinese market	2.12	0.22	
	I can quickly locate supporting industries for sales channels and marketing bases in China	2.34	0.36	
	I can quickly establish a good reputation for Taiwanese agricultural and fishery products in China	3.78	0.48	
	I can overcome the problem of preservation of fresh agricultural and fishery products during shipping	3.91	0.52	
	I can provide processed agricultural and fishery products favored by the Chinese market	3.87	0.41	
	The image and packaging of our agricultural and fishery products are favored by Chinese consumers	3.76	0.52	
Investment intention	I intend to use existing sales channels in China	3.98	0.34	0.868
	I intend to allow investments by Chinese companies in my newly established company	2.87	0.42	
	I intend to directly establish new sales channels and marketing bases in China	4.12	0.23	

4.2 *Factors Affecting the Decision of Taiwanese Entrepreneurs to Establish Marketing Channels in China*

The author conducted a multiple regression analysis to gain a better understanding of whether or not variables pertaining to the background of the respondents (total capital, employee numbers, business categories, and public listing) and psychological variables (attitude, subjective norms, perceived behavior control) have an impact on the intention of Taiwanese entrepreneurs to establish marketing channels in China.

Before conducting the multiple regression analysis, the three items pertaining to investment intention [(1) I intend to use existing sales channels in China. (2) I intend to allow investments by Chinese companies in my newly established company. (3) I intend to directly establish new sales channels and marketing bases in China] were added up to obtain the mean and individual scores were replaced with the mean value. The same method was utilized for the attitude and perceived behavior control items.

Ajzen argues in the description of his theory that subjective norms can be divided into two components, namely normative beliefs and motivation to comply. The measurement of subjective norms is accomplished through the total sum of the products of the normative beliefs and motivation to comply of individuals. The author therefore multiplied the score for "I think the government will provide us with support and advice" by the score for "The provision of support by the government will affect my decision to expand into the Chinese market" and so forth for the remaining items. These four products were added up to obtain the mean and individual scores were replaced with the mean value.

The background variables were converted into dummy variables with two possible values in the following manner: total capital (0 for less than 10 million NTD, 1 for more than 10 million NTD), business categories (0 for agriculture and fishery, 1 for commerce and service industry), employee numbers (0 for less than 50, 1 for 51 and more), and public listing (0 for TPEx listing, 1 for TWSE listing).

The results clearly indicate that perceived behavior control ($\beta = 0.568$), attitude ($\beta = 0.308$), and employee numbers ($\beta = 0.160$) has a significant impact on the intention of Taiwanese entrepreneurs to establish marketing channels in China. The explanatory power of the whole regression model is 0.549. The results therefore reveal that the more sufficient the capabilities and resources for the establishment of marketing channels as perceived by Taiwanese entrepreneurs, the more positive the perception of the Chinese market, and the higher the number of employees, the higher is the intention to make an investment (Table 3).

5 Discussion

5.1 Taiwanese Entrepreneurs Have a Positive View on the Establishment of Marketing Channels in China and High Values Were Recorded for All Psychological Variables with the Sole Exception of Perceived Behavior Control

According to the results of the descriptive statistics analysis, the highest mean value was recorded for the attitude dimension ($M = 3.95$), followed by investment

Table 3 Summary of the regression analysis of factors affecting the intention of Taiwanese entrepreneurs to make investments in China

	Non-standardized coefficients		Standardized coefficients	t	Significance
	Estimated B-value	Standard error	Beta distribution		
(Constants)	−0.189	0.379		−0.498	0.619
Attitude	0.408	0.116	0.308	3.509	0.001**
Subjective norms	0.002	0.014	0.015	0.140	0.888
Perceived behavior control	0.533	0.110	0.568	4.827	0.000***
Total capital	−0.001	0.002	−0.008	−0.303	0.762
Number of employees	0.097	0.043	0.160	2.221	0.027*
Business category	0.001	0.040	0.000	0.018	0.986
Public listing	1.670E−006	0.000	0.070	1.291	0.198
F value	88.453				
Significance	0.000***				
R^2	0.549				

*$p < 0.05$, **$p < 0.01$, ***$p < 0.001$

intention (M = 3.66) and subjective norms (M = 3.47). The lowest value was recorded for perceived behavior control (M = 3.17). On the whole, the respondents have a positive view on the establishment of marketing channels in China and show a strong intention to make investments on the other side of the Strait. It is worth mentioning that the mean value for perceived behavior control on the part of Taiwanese entrepreneurs is comparatively low. The main reason for this phenomenon lies in the low mean values of items including search for marketing channels and bases in China, application for capital loans, recruitment of new employees, understanding of laws and regulations, and location of relevant persons and supporting industries as perceived by Taiwanese entrepreneurs. The mean values for all of these items are below 3, with the sole exception of recruitment of new employees. This clearly indicates that Taiwanese entrepreneurs believe that it is difficult for them to search for marketing channels in China, apply for capital loans, get a better understanding of local laws, contact relevant persons, and locate supporting industries. Based on these findings, the author offers the following suggestion: If the government wishes to increase the intention to establish marketing channels in China and stimulate concrete action on the part of Taiwanese entrepreneurs, it should establish contact points in northern, central, and southern Taiwan for the foundation of companies in China and provide professional consultation services with regard to marketing channels, laws and regulations, and capital loans in a unified manner.

5.2 Perceived Behavior Control, Attitude, and Employee Numbers Have a Significant Impact on the Intention of Taiwanese Entrepreneurs to Establish Marketing Channels in China

The results of the multiple regression analysis clearly show that perceived behavior control has the greatest effect on the decision of Taiwanese entrepreneurs to establish marketing channels in China. The discussion above also indicates that Taiwanese entrepreneurs are highly confident about aspects under their own control such as the rapid establishment of a good reputation for Taiwanese agricultural and fishery products, the satisfaction of demands for preservation of fresh agricultural and fishery products during shipping, the manufacture of processed agricultural and fishery products favored by the Chinese market, and the provision of agricultural and fishery products whose image and packaging are favored by Chinese consumers. However, they tend to have reservations or lack confidence in their ability to find marketing channels in China, meet important persons for marketing channels, gain a deeper understanding of laws and regulations, and apply for capital loans. Attitude and employee numbers also have a significant impact on investment intention. This in turn indicates that Taiwanese entrepreneurs show a higher intention to make an investment on the other side of the Strait if they agree that the establishment of marketing bases in China is a general trend, China is the largest market in the vicinity of Taiwan, Taiwanese entrepreneurs enjoy an advantage when making investments in China due to the same language and ethnicity, China is located in the vicinity of Taiwan, Chinese consumers favor agricultural and fishery products from Taiwan, and Taiwanese businesses enjoy preferential terms in China. Finally, companies with more than 51 employees tend to be more inclined to make investments in China than companies with less than 50 employees.

5.3 The Government Should Establish Contact Points for Consultation in Taipei, Taichung, and Kaohsiung

The results of the questionnaire survey indicate that the majority of Taiwanese entrepreneurs believe that the Taiwanese government is currently encouraging them to make investments in China. However, the government has so far failed to set up contact points for consultation on investments in China. Taiwanese entrepreneurs are therefore forced to consult the opinions of entrepreneurs who have experience with investments in China or are currently investing in the Chinese market. However, their experiences are not uniform and they are engaged in different industries. These experiences are therefore hard to replicate and may not be applied to their circumstances. Consequently, the respondents generally expect the government to set up contact points for consultation in Taipei, Taichung, and

Kaohsiung or organize regular information meetings on investments in China to provide Taiwanese entrepreneurs who intend to expand into the Chinese market and make investments on the other side of the Strait with a deeper understanding of the Chinese market and local laws and regulations.

References

Ajzen I (1988) Attitudes, personality and behavior. The Dorsey Press, Chicago

Ajzen I (1991) The theory of planned behavior. Organ Behav Hum Decis Process 50:179

Ajzen I, Madden TJ (1986) Prediction of goal-directed behavior: attitudes, intentions, and perceived behavioral control. J Exper Soc Psychol 22:453

Armitage CJ, Conner M (2001) Efficacy of the theory of planned behaviour: a meta-analytic review. Br J Soc Psychol 40:471

Ceren T, Dilek SK, Elvan S (2011) A study on teacher candidates' recycling behaviors: a model approach with the theory of planned behaviour. West Anatolia J Edu Sci (**special issue**) 29

Chu PY, Chiu JF (2003) Factors influencing household waste recycling behavior:test of an integrated model. J Appl Soc Psychol 33:604

Council of Agriculture (2015) ECFA FAQ http://www.coa.gov.tw/view.php?catid=21309

Fishbein M (1980) A theory of reasoned action: Some applications and implications. In: Howe H, Page M (eds) Nebraska symposium on motivation. University of Nebraska Press, Lincoln

Hartmann P, Apaolaza-Ibanez V (2008) Virtual nature experiences as emotional benefits in green product consumption: the moderating role of environmental attitudes. Environ Behav 40:818

Hines JM, Hungerford HR, Tomera AN (1986) Analysis and synthesis of research on responsible environmental behavior: a meta- analysis. J Environ Edu 18:1

Hwang YH, Kim SI, Jeng JM (2000) Examining the causal relationships among selected antecedents of responsible environmental behavior. J Environ Edu 31:19

Lai SY, Qian SQ, Cai FL (2013) Analysis of the intention of tourists to visit a museum by employing the theory of planned behavior- A case study of the Kaohsiung museum of fine arts. Asia Pac Econ Manage Rev 16:39

Li YM, Qiu YW, Shi DH (2005) Empirical comparative study of conflicting usage tendency modes of online learning. NTU Manage Rev 16:41

Lin WB, Yang SF (2005) Analysis of usage intention modes affecting the online learning market: application of the fuzzy neural network method. Sun Yat-sen Manage Rev 13:721

Shen SD, Qiu HY (2014) Factors affecting the willingness of university faculty and staff members to adopt eco-friendly behavior patterns—a case study of a university in northern Taiwan. J Des Sci 17:71

Tu PQ, Xu WY, Zhang ZX, Chen YR (2011) Assessment of the intention of outpatient cancer patients to participate in psychological and social intervention—application of the theory of planned behavior. Formosa J Mental Health 24:403

Wang YW, Ke HL, Yan YY, Lin YZ, Lin BL, Hu ZY, Huang XL (2013) Application of the theory of planned behavior to explore factors affecting the intention of teenagers to give up smoking—a case study of a certain nursing college in southern Taiwan. Taiwan J Oral Med Sci 28:4

Wu MF (2011) Analysis of the factors affecting the intention of farmers to engage in organic agriculture by employing the theory of planned behavior. Dissertation, Institute of Public Affairs Management, National Sun Yat-sen University

Does Strategic Planning Influence Synergy and Therefore a Firm's Performance? An Empirical Study at Selected Manufacturing Companies in Indonesia

Augustinus Nicolaas Hillebrandes Oroh

Abstract This research aims to examine the impact of relatedness and sharing on a firm's synergy, strategic planning on synergy, and on the firm's overall performance. The study used descriptive research design. The mediating role of strategic planning is explored whether it will support a positive influence on the implementation of synergy toward a firm's performance. The conceptual framework was tested using a multiple regression model. Data was collected using questionnaires distributed to senior managers, general managers, and directors of selective manufacturing companies in Indonesia. The hypotheses were analyzed using IBM SPSS. The results suggest that not only does strategic planning have a direct impact to firm's performance but also on its synergy. Strategic planning involving synergy also has an influence on a firm's performance. In support of past findings, the present study shows either sharing or relatedness (or both) of a firm's resources lends strong support to synergy, synergy supports strategic planning and the overall performance of the firm.

Keywords Sharing · Relatedness · Synergy · Strategic planning · Firm performance

1 Introduction and Theoretical Background

One of the most common strategic activities to combine a firm's operation and strategies is synergy. Synergy word comes from Greece *synergos* meaning "*working together*" (Hitt et al. 2005). Synergy has been defined as occurring when more value is created by a combined performance between firm units compared to if the units

A.N.H. Oroh (✉)
Business Management and Marketing Program, Bina Nusantara University, Jakarta, Indonesia
e-mail: Nico@binus.edu
URL: http://www.international.binus.ac.id

S. Soh (ed.), *Selected Papers from the Asia Conference on Economics & Business Research 2015*, DOI 10.1007/978-981-10-0986-0_9

worked by themselves. Webster's New World Dictionary describes "synergy" as combined or cooperative action or force (Neufeldt and Guralnik 1996).

When exploring Ansoff's view of the strategy and synergy model, Mintzberg said synergy as a concept subsequently became so popular in management that it probably stands as Ansoff's most sustained contribution (Mintzberg 1994). Conversely, in the footnote of a book on the same theme, Mintzberg said that synergy is mentioned in a 1962 paper by other authors who credited Ansoff with the term.

Synergy as an activity may become a starting point to explain and to ensure firms not only have been doing the right things but also doing things right. However, many scholars still argue whether synergy is really beneficial to top performing firms. Research on what variables really affect synergy and the impact of having it as a firm's main focus (which might positively enhance a firm's performance) could then become a method with which to give more attention to its strategic value.

Top performing firms strive to maintain and sustain their competitive advantages by innovating the way they respond to their customer's needs and to stay on top of the competition. These firms explore opportunities to introduce more new products and services and then to create a much shorter product life cycle to stay ahead of the competition, and therefore ensure competitive advantage.

Global turbulence in industry has forced firm's top management and academics to be very careful in examining the real cause of a firm's performance. Some scholars are focusing their studies on the external impact of the firm environments which include the environmental turbulence, competitors' strategies, government constraints (Ansoff and McDonnell 1990; Hitt et al. 2009) while others are exploring firm's internal problems as the main issues, like improper value chain analysis and activities, lack of strategic planning and leadership, business unit's coordination problems, or a shortage of strategic managers (Steiner 1979; Ansoff 1988; Porter 1983, 1985).

Balancing those strategic activities has become one of the key success factors in top performing firms. On one hand firms must focus on the internal concerns to ensure low costs, and to produce acceptable products or services in the eyes of their loyal and potential customers. On the other hand, they have to ensure their readiness to be always on top of a situation during turbulent and unpredictable conditions. Firms have to ensure their overall strategic aggressiveness and general management capabilities align with today's and future's turbulence levels to stay competitive (Ansoff and McDonnell 1990).

1.1 Sharing

Firms practitioners have been using the term "sharing" as "dividing resources to other business unit(s)", and if properly planned would have many strategic benefits to the overall firm performance (Ansoff 1990; Porter 1983, 1985, Steiner 1979).

Scholars argue that:

> The basis for synergy is sharing of resources across business activities. These may be geographic markets, product lines, customer groups, and so on. However, sharing is a necessary but not sufficient condition for synergy. In some situations, the resources being shared may not have the potential for synergy. In other situations, the potential synergy is not fully realized. Finally, realized synergy may not always lead to a sustainable competitive advantage for the firm (Gruca et al. 1997).

On the other hand other researchers found that employee's sharing capability (Jalal et al. 2013), explicit and tacit knowledge sharing practices (Wang and Wang 2012), improving information sharing and trust (Abdullah and Musa 2014) will support companies to remain competitive.

From the above point of views we can argue that sharing if it really correctly understands and properly executes may have a relationship with synergy for any company.

1.2 Relatedness

The word "relate" is synonymous with "connect" or "link" or "form a relationship" (Oxford English Dictionary). Supportive connected activities will provide a mutually beneficial relationship between firms, business units, and departments who conduct them and will therefore increase competitive advantage.

Relatedness refers to the degree to which business units support or complement each other's business activities, particularly marketing and production. It is the mechanism by which businesses capture synergies that can enhance their competitive advantage relative to their competitors (Davis et al. 1992). The authors quoted from Porter (1985) said that business units that effectively capitalize on relatedness may be able to use interrelationships to overwhelm single business competitors or competitors with poorly conceived arrays of business units.

Businesses are said to be related when their value chains exhibit or demonstrate competitively important cross-business relationships, which means there is a close correlation between the businesses in terms of how they perform key value chain activities and the resources and capabilities each needs to perform those activities (Thompson et al. 2014). The question is whether the firm's management has the capability to coordinate those activities without having formal planning especially for multinational companies operating in many countries where different markets need unique and special skills.

Based on the above point of views we can say that the more relatedness a company has within its departments or business units will additionally affect its overall synergy.

1.3 Synergy

The study of synergy has been in progress for many years and has showed both positive and negative impacts on a firm's performance (Gruca et al. 1997).

Politicians have frequently suggested that in order to succeed and to create competitive advantage in a turbulence business environment, state-owned enterprises need to synergize within and between themselves by implementing obvious and clear synergy activities, indicators, and performance measurements.

Scholars have developed a framework for companies that wish to conduct a management audit of how well their approach to synergy management is working. The framework, which has been used successfully by several companies, provides a practical and systematic way of pinpointing unrealized opportunities and creating an agenda of initiatives for addressing them (Goold and Campbell 1998).

Increasing profitability via synergy requires a selective focus on management synergy, sales, and certain aspects of the operations synergy. The specific synergy dimension of value in order to increase ROI differs greatly by the type of business involved. Thus, increased profitability, via synergy, requires design and implementation of a synergy analysis and strategy program (Mahajan and Wind 1988).

The research at Samsung finds that noneconomic influences prevailed over economic influences in the decision to pursue diversification strategy. Due in part to the strength of these influences, Samsung underestimated the market risk and overestimated the contribution its core competencies and synergy could make (Lee and Lee 2007).

We can argue that company who has more synergy in its activities will have better firm's performance.

1.4 Strategic Planning

A basic theory of management says that planning is the first activity any organization needs to manage its resources efficiently and effectively to achieve its goals. This activity needs to be officially discussed and put into official documents to become organizational guidance, and therefore a formal plan.

According to Ansoff (1990, 1991), the key contextual variable is the concept of environmental turbulence which is actually an elaboration of the concepts of unpredictability and uncertainty used by Mintzberg 1994. In Ansoff research, five distinctive levels of observable environmental turbulence were identified, ranging from stable to creative. For the purposes of identification of context it is useful to aggregate turbulence levels into two categories: (1) *Incremental turbulence* in which environmental changes are a logical evolution of the historical change process, and the speed of the changes is slower than the response time of the organizations; and (2) *Discontinuous turbulence* in which successive changes are discontinuous from the preceding ones, and speed of change is greater than the speed of the organizations' response. Following this argument, a company's plan

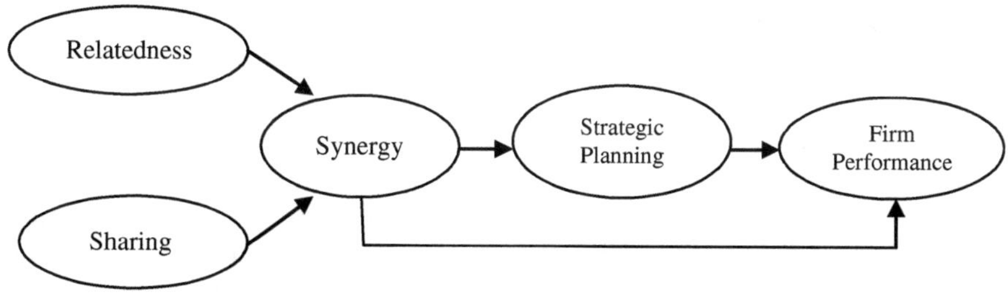

Fig. 1 Framework/research model based on hypotheses

therefore should be strategically aligned with the environmental turbulence level and also formally established by the top management.

More studies in strategic planning have been conducted with results suggesting a positive relationship with a firm's performance. Even with mediating variables in between, including: innovativeness—which fully mediates the relationship between firm performance and formal strategic planning process and flexibility (Dibrell et al. 2014); dual performance effects of strategic planning and autonomous actions on a firm's performance (Andersen 2000); four types of strategic planning flexibility to firm's performance (Rudd et al. 2008); and strategic planning system of strategy formulation, decision-making, and control from particular planning technologies such as Strategic Business Unit planning toward a firm's performance (Ocasio and Wechallenge 2008).

From the above point of views we can strongly argue that the more strategic planning used by a company the better the overall performance should be.

1.5 Firm Performance

Owners and leaders need to measure if their firms are performing according to the stated objectives or not. Scholars argue whether financial statements alone are enough for firm's leaders to make further strategic decisions for the future of the companies to ensure their competitive advantage.

Accordingly many mix of nonfinancial and financial performance measures have been used recently by scholars in their current research. New product launches, market development and penetration, quality improvement, and customer satisfaction combined with a firm's sales growth, profitability, and return on investment have all been investigated (Wang et al. 2015) against the conventional financial return on sales, growth in profit, return on assets, sales growth, market share growth, and cash flow (Gonzales et al. 2015).

Furthermore other researchers are measuring firm performance by using nonfinancial indicators when respondents were asked to rate the degree to which survey questions are a current concern to their companies, as compared to the industry average (Feng et al. 2013) (Fig. 1).

2 Research Methodology

All variables including relatedness, sharing, synergy, strategic planning, and firm performance. In general a Likert scale from 1 ("strongly disagreed or poor") to 5 ("strongly agreed or extensive") was used to measure those questions. Questionnaires were sent to more than 100 management members including senior managers, general managers, and to the director's level of manufacturing companies in Indonesia, e.g., pulp and paper, automotive, chemical, pharmaceutical, fertilizer, and infrastructure. A pretest was conducted prior to sending those questionnaires to ensure all respondents clearly understood the meaning of each question by asking them directly through emails, phone calls, and discussions.

Since there are more than two predictors included in the proposed model the author used the multiple linear regression analysis to ascertain whether the framework was statistically significant and acceptable. In order to extend and examine further, a simple mediation analysis was utilized in which the variables were arranged in a predictive causal path model to assess the dynamics of their interplay (Meyers et al. 2013).

2.1 Measurement

2.1.1 Relatedness

Scholars used market and production relatedness by capturing questions about the extent to which customers, sales force, and advertisement and promotion were shared. Production relatedness was captured by questions about the extent to which business units shared plants and equipment, R&D, or had interdivisional product transfers (Davis et al. 1992).

2.1.2 Sharing

Following previous research on manufacturing and operation, sharing can be measured by determining the degree of sharing resources in a company by several departments (Mahajan and Wind 1988). Original questionnaires were designed using a Likert scale from 1 ("strongly agreed") to 5 ("strongly disagreed") and have been modified for the purpose of this study.

From the original question researcher has explored further and divided into more understandable questions such as: did your company share its manufacturing plant with another department; did your company share its operating plant with another department; did your company share its equipment facilities with another department; did your company share its personnel with another department?

2.1.3 Synergy

Following earlier research and the respondent's background in manufacturing companies, measuring synergy can be done by analyzing sales activities and operation activities (Mahajan and Wind 1988). Questions are focused on the customers, sales force, advertising program, sales promotion program, and to whether the purchase of materials, and supplies were obtained from other companies of the same group. A Likert scale has been used.

2.1.4 Strategic Planning

This variable is measured using the model from the study that explores the link between financial performance and the formal strategic planning process, planning flexibility, and innovativeness of 448 firms in a multi-industry sample (Dibrell et al. 2014). For the formal strategic planning process the original Likert scale was from 1 (none or not at all) to 5 (to an extreme extent) and for Planning flexibility from 1 (not all flexible or a trigger) to 5 (very flexible or a definite trigger).

2.1.5 Firm Performance

A firm performance can be measured by analyzing the normal and standard financial statement, namely the firm's income statement, balance sheet, and cash flow statement. However, more and more nonfinancial measures have been used by researchers to analyze a firm's performance. The author is referring to the model in which all respondents were asked to rate the degree to which the survey questions are a current concern to their companies, as compared to the industry average. The original model used a 7-point Likert scale with 1 for strongly disagreed and 7 for strongly agreed (Feng et al. 2013), but to be consistent with the other variables the researcher modified the scale to 1 for strongly disagreed and 5 for strongly agreed.

3 Results

From the IBM SPSS statistical analysis ANOVA table presented below it is clear that the research model accounts for a significant amount of dependent variable variance. Prior to analyzing the mediating role of strategic planning on the relationship between synergy and firm performance, the author has tested the relationship between two independent variables "sharing" and "relatedness" to synergy as a dependent variable (Figs. 2 and 3).

Descriptive Statistics

	Mean	Std. Deviation	N
Synergy	3.653	.2497	110
Relatedness	4.016	.5788	110
Sharing	3.224	.9942	110

Fig. 2 The descriptive statistics test results of synergy, relatedness, and sharing

Model Summary

Model	R	R Square	Adjusted R Square	Std. Error of the Estimate	Change Statistics				
					R Square Change	F Change	df1	df2	Sig. F Change
1	.801[a]	.642	.635	.1508	.642	95.898	2	107	.000

a. Predictors: (Constant), Sharing, Relatedness

Coefficients[a]

Model		Unstandardized Coefficients		Standardized Coefficients	T	Sig.	Correlations		
		B	Std. Error	Beta			Zero-order	Partial	Part
1	(Constant)	2.222	.105		21.203	.000			
	Relatedness	.432	.034	1.001	12.891	.000	.751	.780	.746
	Sharing	-.094	.020	-.375	-4.833	.000	.293	-.423	-.280

a. Dependent Variable: Synergy

ANOVA[a]

Model		Sum of Squares	Df	Mean Square	F	Sig.
1	Regression	4.361	2	2.181	95.898	.000[b]
	Residual	2.433	107	.023		
	Total	6.794	109			

a. Dependent Variable: Synergy

Fig. 3 The model summary, coefficients, and ANOVA tables using relatedness and sharing to predict synergy

Descriptive Statistics

	Mean	Std. Deviation	N
FPerformance	3.667	.3970	110
Synergy	3.653	.2497	110

Fig. 4 The descriptive statistics test results of firm performance and synergy

Based on the analysis results synergy has a statistically significant correlation with relatedness and sharing, and especially with relatedness as it has a positive and higher correlation to synergy than sharing. The higher the degree of relatedness, the more positive relationship it has with synergy, and this can be seen at the high positive coefficient correlation.

As mentioned earlier the author is using a simple mediation tool to analyze further whether strategic planning has mediated the relationship between synergy and firm's performance. The ANOVA table provides a test result of the statistical significance of the regression model. The author's proposed model accounts for a significant amount of dependent variables variance (Sig. 0.000). The model is statistically significant (Figs. 4 and 5).

Furthermore by using the simple mediation path analysis (Meyers et al. 2013) the author can determine the relative strength of strategic planning mediating effect on the relationship between synergy and firm performance by calculating the ratio of the strength of the indirect effect to the strength of the direct effect. The calculation is as follows:

The beta coefficients associated with paths of synergy to strategic planning and from strategic planning to firm performance in the mediated model is equal to $(0.332) \times (0.467) = 0.155$.

The beta coefficient in the unmediated model where synergy is the single predictor of firm performance stated in the table at 0.249.

The relative strength is equal to the indirect effect divided by the direct effect which is $0.155/0.249 = 0.6224$.

Based on the above formula we can then conclude that about 62.24 % of the effect of synergy to firm performance is mediated through strategic planning.

Variables Entered/Removed[a]

Model	Variables Entered	Variables Removed	Method
1	Synergy[b]	.	Enter

a. Dependent Variable: FPerformance
b. All requested variables entered.

Model Summary

Model	R	R Square	Adjusted R Square	Std. Error of the Estimate	Change Statistics				
					R Square Change	F Change	df1	df2	Sig. F Change
1	.249[a]	.062	.053	.3863	.062	7.136	1	108	.009

a. Predictors: (Constant), Synergy

ANOVA[a]

Model		Sum of Squares	Df	Mean Square	F	Sig.
1	Regression	4.404	2	2.202	18.437	.000[b]
	Residual	12.779	107	.119		
	Total	17.182	109			

a. Dependent Variable: FPerformance
b. Predictors: (Constant), StrategicPlanning, Synergy

Correlations

		FPerformance	Synergy
Pearson Correlation	FPerformance	1.000	.249
	Synergy	.249	1.000
Sig. (1-tailed)	FPerformance	.	.004
	Synergy	.004	.
N	FPerformance	110	110
	Synergy	110	110

Fig. 5 The model summary, ANOVA, and correlations test results using strategic planning and synergy to predict firm performance

3.1 Managerial Implications

Synergy, statistically proven, has a positive relationship with firm performance. Companies with more understanding of synergy will have a better overall performance than its competitors who have no any idea about it (Ansoff 1988, 1990;

Mahajan et al. 1988; Porter 1983; Damodaran 2005). Synergy can become a source of competitive advantage during turbulent environments, intense competition and where company's activities are becoming more and more similar.

From this finding, synergy needs to be clearly understood by all managers at firms' strategic business units and seriously formulated by the top management to support and achieve a better overall performance. Sharing and relatedness compositions and indicators should be intentionally discussed and general management has to ensure these strategic aspects will be the Key Performance Indicators (KPI) of each business unit head, department head, and all firm leaders. Furthermore a strategic plan needs to be explicitly formulated, established, and implemented by all units, departments, and other firm strategic business units.

From this research relatedness has been the main variable for synergy and the use of cross-functional teams in the new product development is a major indicator of relatedness. Thus, companies need to ensure that cross-functional team aspects will be taken care of by managing and allocating sufficient resources and maintaining the effectiveness of coordination. Failure to focus will reduce the overall synergy effectiveness and accordingly the firm's performance.

Strategic planning, statistically proven, is the answer to increase the firm's performance which supports previous research (Steiner 1979; Ansoff 1970, 1990, 1991; Dibrell et al. 2014). Companies who fail to establish strategic planning will have less bargaining position and power to compete against established rivals and potential competitors (Lee and Lee 2007; Ocasio and Wechallenge 2008).

Based on the findings top management needs to focus on enumerating objectives as bold and clear as possible to the management team and then to ensure strategy implementation plans is the result of the strategy formation process. Management team has to communicate the outcome as transparently as possible to the business units to control proper execution.

Furthermore attention should be given to the firms' future growth environment with new market needs, new products or service technologies, and new geographical areas. Firms should assign people with strategic management skills who will be responsible to initiate and complete the strategic planning sessions since these will be crucial for firms to create different activities than their competitors. Thus assigning key managers with strategic management skills to become the person responsible is critical to ensure strategic plan implementation for achieving a firm's superior performance.

A further study on the role of general management and chief executive officers in establishing strategic plans should be conducted to confirm whether their strategic positions are undeniably ensuring implementation to create firm sustainable competitive advantage.

3.2 *Limitations and Future Research*

Several points can be included for future research such as more data to be collected from different countries around South East Asia or outside Indonesia. In order to gain better and deeper managerial insights, more experienced strategic managers, e.g., chief executive officers, chief operating officers, and chief marketing officers need to be interviewed and incorporated in the research.

Acknowledgments The author would like to thank the United States International University and Alliant International University library in San Diego, California, U.S.A. for their support by providing several research hard copies conducted by the late distinguished Professor Igor Ansoff "the father of strategic management" and his fellow students at the Igor Ansoff School of Strategic Management.

References

Abdullah Z, Musa R (2014) The effect of trust and information sharing on relationship commitment in supply chain management. Procedia Soc Behav Sci 130:266–272

Andersen TJ (2000) Strategic planning, autonomous actions and corporate performance. Long Range Plan 33:184–200

Ansoff HI, Avner J, Brandenburg RG, Portner FE, Radosevich R (1970) Does planning pay? The effect of planning on success of acquisitions in American firms. Long Range Plan

Ansoff HI, (1988) The new corporate strategy, John Wiley & Sons, Inc., New York. (Published originally as Corporate Strategy, New York: McGraw-Hill, 1965)

Ansoff HI, McDonnell E (1990) Implanting strategic management, 2nd edn. Prentice Hall International, Cambridge

Ansoff HI (1991) Critique of Henry Mintzberg "The Design School" reconsidering the basic premises of strategic management. Strateg Manag J vol 12

Bonn I, Christodoulou C (1996) From strategic planning to strategic management. Long Range Plan 29(4):543–551

Carter JR (1977) In search of synergy a structure-performance test. Rev Econ Stat 59(3)

Cohen JF, Olsen K (2015) Knowledge management capabilities and firm performance: A test of universalistic, contingency and complementarity perspectives. Expert Syst Appl 42:1178–1188

Damodaran, A (2005), The value of synergy. Stern School of Business, New York

Davis PS, Robinson RB, Pearce JA, Park SH (1992) Business unit relatedness and performance: A look at the pulp and paper industry. Strateg Manag J 13:349–361

Dibrell C, Craig JB, Neubaum DO (2014) Linking the formal strategic planning process, planning flexibility, and innovativeness to firm performance. J Bus Res 67:2000–2007

Fan JPH, Lang LHP (2000) The measurement of relatedness: an application to corporate diversification. J Bus 73(4):629–660

Feng T, Li T, Sun L, & Wang D (2013) External involvement and operational performance: the mediating role of internal integration. Emerald Group Publishing Limited, Chin Manage Stud 7 (3):488–507

Fluck Z, Lynch AW (1999) Why do firms merge and then divest? A theory of financial synergy. J Bus 72(3):319–346

Flynn BB, Huo B, Zhao X (2010) The impact of supply chain integration on performance: a contingency and configuration approach. J Oper Manage 28:58–71

Gonzales JC, Saez PL, Lopez JEN, Verde, MD (2015) Open search strategies and firm performance: the different moderating role of technological environmental dynamism. Technovation 35:32–45
Goold M, & Campbell A (1998) Desperately seeking synergy. Harvard Business Review, Boston
Gruca TS, Nath D, Mehra AJ (1997) Exploiting synergy for competitive advantage. Long Range Plan 30(4):605–611
Hanssens DM, Johansson JK (1991) Rivalry as synergy? The Japanese automobile companies' export expansion. J Int Bus Stud 22(3):503–526
Hitt M, Ireland D, Hoskisson R (2005) Strategic management, 6th edn. Thomson South-Western, Ohio
Hitt MA, King D, Krishnan H, Makri M, Schijven M, Shimizu K, Zhu H (2009) Mergers and acquisitions: overcoming pitfalls, building synergy, and creating value. Bus Horiz 52:523–529
Huang CT, Tsai KH (2014) Synergy environmental context, and new product performance: a review based on manufacturing firms. Ind Market Manage 43:1407–1419
Jalal HA, Toulson P, Tweed D (2013) Knowledge sharing success for sustaining organizational competitive advantage. Procedia Econ Financ 7:150–157
Kalkana A, Ersoy MA (2013) The choice and use of strategic planning tools and techniques in Turkish SMEs according to attitudes of executives. Procedia Soc Behav Sci 99:1016–1025
Kollman T, Kuckerts A, Kayser I (2012) Cannibalization or synergy? Consumers' channel selection in online–offline multichannel systems. J Retail Consum Serv 19:186–194
Lee W, Lee NS (2007) Understanding Samsung's diversification strategy: the case of Samsung Motors Inc. Long Range Plan 40:488–504
Li L, Qian G, Qian Z (2013) Do partners in international strategic alliances share resources, costs, and risks? J Bus Res 66:489–498
Mahajan V, Wind Y (1988) Business synergy does not always pay off. Long Range Plan 21(1)
Matzler K, Mueller J (2011) Antecedents of knowledge sharing—examining the influence of learning and performance orientation. J Econ Psychol 32:317–329
Meyers LS, Gamst GC, Guarion AJ (2013) Performing data analysis using IBM SPSS. Wiley, New Jersey
Mintzberg H (1994) The rise and fall of strategic planning: reconceiving roles for planning, plans, planners. The Free Press, A Division of Simon & Schuster Inc., New York 10020
Naik PA, Peters KA (2009) Hierarchical marketing communications model of online and offline media synergies. J Interact Market 23:288–299
Neufeldt V, & Guralnik DB (1996) Webster's new world college dictionary, Macmillan general reference. A Simon & Schuster Macmillan Company, Broadway, New York
Ocasio W, Wechallenge JJ (2008) Rise and fall—or transformation? the evolution of strategic planning at the general electric company, 1940–2006. Long Range Plan 41:248–272
Park K, Jang S (2013) Effects of within-industry diversification and related diversification strategies on firm performance. Int J Hospitality Manage 34:51–60
Porter ME (1983) Industrial organization and the evolution of concepts for strategic planning: the new learning. Manag Decis Econ 4(3)
Porter ME (1985) Competitive advantage, creating and sustaining superior performance. The Free Press, New York
Rozemeijer F (2000) How to manage corporate purchasing synergy in a decentralized company? Towards design rules for managing and organising purchasing synergy in decentralised companies. Eur J Purchasing Supply Manage 6(5):12
Rudd JM, Greenley GE, Beatson AT, Lings IN (2008) Strategic planning and performance: extending the debate. J Bus Res 61:99–108
Steiner GA (1979) Strategic planning, what every manager must know. New York, Free Press Paperbacks
Theodosiou M, Kehagias J, Katsikea E (2012) Strategic orientations, marketing capabilities and firm performance: an empirical investigation in the context of frontline managers in service organizations. Ind Mark Manage 41:1058–1070

Thompson AA, Peteraf MA, Gamble JE, Strickland III AJ (2014) Crafting and executing strategy. The Quest For Competitive Advantage, Concepts and Cases, 19th edn. McGraw-Hill Education

Wang Z, Wang N (2012) Knowledge sharing, innovation and firm performance. Expert Syst Appl 39(2012):8899–8908

Wang G, Dou W, Zhu W, Zhou N (2015) The effect of firm capabilities on external collaboration and performance: the moderating role of market turbulence, J of Bus Res

Weigand K, Flanagan T, Dye K, Jones P (2014) Collaborative foresight: complementing long-horizon strategic planning. Technol Forecast Soc Chang 85:134–152

Income Distribution and the 2008–2012 Economic Crisis: The Latin American Experience

Mario Iván Domínguez Rivas and Benjamín García Páez

Abstract This paper analyses the financial and economic crises that had a differentiated impact in the Latin-American region, depending on the ability of some countries to keep up an aggregate demand—i.e., through redistribution devices like the degree of integration held within the foreign financial sector. Based on a sample of regional economies, and working over a period spanning from 2000 to 2013, we found that countries with a relatively better income distribution and domestic financial systems connected with credit programs supporting consumption and investment, had had a better economic performance than those countries with a strong linkage to the international financial system, given that the crisis was ignited at the banking system and accelerated by the same mechanism over-spreading negative shock effects on their capacity to offset them and, in doing so, try an economic recovery. Finally, the authors raise some hints to devise correct policy changes to deal in the still aftermath of the crises in Latin America from a post Keynesian perspective.

Keywords Income distribution · Gini coefficient · Financial deepening · Market capitalization · Re-industrialization risks and re-industrialization projects

1 Income Distribution and Growth in Latin America

In a context of global financial crisis, such as the one occurred in 2008–2009, a strong integration into the global financial system is a source of infection for the economies of different countries.

M.I. Domínguez Rivas (✉)
Instituto Belisario Domínguez, Senado de la República, 06020 Mexico City, Mexico
e-mail: ivandie@live.com

B. García Páez
Professor in Economics of Growth and Development Economic,
National Autonomous University of Mexico, University City, Mexico City, Mexico
e-mail: garpaez@unam.mx

S. Soh (ed.), *Selected Papers from the Asia Conference on Economics & Business Research 2015*, DOI 10.1007/978-981-10-0986-0_10

Table 1 GINI index

Year/country	Bolivia	Brazil	Chile	Colombia	Ecuador	Mexico	Venezuela
2000	0.643	n.a.	0.564	n.a.	0.559	0.542	0.468
2003	n.a.	0.621	0.552	0.548	n.a.	n.a.	n.a.
2006	n.a.	0.605	0.522	n.a.	0.527	0.506	0.447
2009	0.508	0.576	0.524	0.553	0.5	n.a.	0.416
2012	n.a.	0.567	n.a.	0.536	n.a.	0.492	0.405
2013	n.a.	0.553	0.509	0.536	0.477	n.a.	0.407

Notes 1 n.a. = not available
Source CEPAL

Some of the factors that may mitigate the effects of this contagion are, on the one hand, the reduction of inequality that can boost growth by raising aggregate demand and, on the other hand, to have an internal system that offers financial services with affordable rates of interest in ways that strengthen aggregate credit through investment and consumption demand. By contrast, a financial system that allocates credit to disproportionately high interest rates generates a negative income redistribution and, eventually, will reduce aggregate demand.

1.1 Income Distribution in Latin America (2000–2013)

In a sample of Latin American economies (see Table 1), the reduction of income inequality is clear, measured through the Gini Index. The country with the biggest breakthrough in the fight against inequality was Bolivia, who drove down 13 points between 2000 and 2009, to continue with a further decline of 4 points in 2011. Then come Ecuador and Brazil, with a reduction in inequality by 6 points during the period 2000–2009. However, Brazil continues to have greater inequality within the countries analyzed. For its part, Colombia slightly reduced its inequality only by one points, while Venezuela maintains the lowest values of the Gini index among the countries selected for the study sample. (See Table 1).

2 Financial System

2.1 Integration into the Global Financial System (2000–2012)

Using the Market capitalization of listed companies (% of GDP),[1] as a degree of integration indicator into the global financial system, it is observed that

[1]Market capitalization (also known as market value) is the share price times the number of shares outstanding. Listed domestic companies are the domestically incorporated companies listed on the

Table 2 Market capitalization of listed countries (% of GDP)

Year/country	Bolivia	Brazil	Chile	Colombia	Ecuador	Mexico	Venezuela
2000	20.74	35.08	76.14	9.57	3.84	18.31	6.94
2003	15.86	42.46	110.86	15.06	6.64	17.18	4.57
2006	19.41	65.30	112.86	34.53	8.63	36.03	4.50
2009	16.10	72.05	121.56	57.01	6.79	38.04	2.69
2012	16.44	54.69	117.68	70.78	7.03	44.25	6.64

Source World bank

participation in the stock market has tended to grow in the national economies under scrutiny. Chile, for example, is the country with the largest capitalization during the period. Brazil is the second country with the largest market capitalization, although it had a significant reduction in 2012. Colombia's capitalization sevenfold from 2000 to 2012, increased from 9.6 to 70.8 % of GDP, and Mexico is more than double that figure in that period; for 2012 it came up to 44.2 %.

The more cautious countries, in terms of stock market capitalization, are Bolivia, Ecuador and Venezuela; Bolivia capitalization decreased 20.7–16.4 % in 2000–2012, while Ecuador and Venezuela are the countries with the lowest level of capitalization, 7.0 and 6.6 % respectively, for the past year. (See Table 2).

2.2 *National Financial Sector*

Using bank credit as an indicator of a share of GDP, and Interest rate spread (IRS) for the behavior of the financial sector in each country, Chile is the country with greater allocation of domestic credit as a percentage of GDP, while Brazil is the country with the greatest differential in interest rate charged to users of the banking system. Venezuela and Mexico are the countries with the lowest differential in the interest rate. (See Table 3).

The granting of domestic credit has increased from 2006 to 2012 in the sampled countries. Mexico, for example, has maintained a steady growth of bank credit granted, reaching 46.7 as a fraction of GDP in 2012. On the other hand, Bolivia has reduced the proportion of loans. Ecuador has the lowest proportion of loans with respect to its GDP for 2012.

(Footnote 1 continued)

country's stock exchanges at the end of the year. Listed companies does not include investment companies, mutual funds, or other collective investment vehicles.

Table 3 Interest rate spread and domestic credit (% of GDP)

Year	2000		2003		2006		2009		2012	
	IRS	Credit as % of GDP	IRS	Credit as % of GDP	IRS	Credit as % of GDP	IRS	Credit as % of GDP	IRS	Credit as % of GDP
Bolivia	23.6	62.0	6.3	58.1	7.9	57.5	8.9	49.5	9.5	48.7
Brazil	39.6	71.9	45.1	74.0	36.9	86.6	35.4	93.1	28.7	110.8
Chile	5.6	78.1	3.4	83.5	2.9	78.7	5.2	105.7	4.3	112.6
Colombia	6.6	30.4	7.4	40.7	6.6	51.7	6.9	62.0	7.2	69.4
Ecuador	8.3	30.6	8.0	14.4	5.6	17.5	n.a.	17.4	n.a.	29.2
Mexico	8.7	29.0	3.9	32.6	4.2	34.3	5.1	43.1	3.6	46.7
Venezuela	8.9	14.9	8.0	10.6	5.2	18.4	3.5	25.9	1.9	48.3

Notes 1 n.a. = not available; *IRS* Interest rate spreads
Source World bank

Table 4 Macroeconomic performance 2008–2012

Country	Reducing inequality	Integration into the global financial system	Domestic credit	Average GDP growth rate (2008–2013)
Bolivia	High	Very Low	High	5.13
Brazil	High	Average	High	3.11
Chile	Low	High	Average	3.89
Colombia	Low	Low	High	4.08
Ecuador	High	Low	Low	4.70
Mexico	Average	High	Average	1.82
Venezuela	High	Low	Low	1.96

Source World bank

3 Results Obtained

Taking into consideration Table 1 and the overall macroeconomic performance shown in Table 4, by including Gini coefficient measured for the degree of inequality in income distribution,[2] which must be considered as an additional endogenous factor, income distribution is good for growth but subjected to the condition that the country in point has a robust banking system prone to fulfill sound intermediation financial functions.

The way that inequality reduction influences growth is through the enhancement of aggregate demand and, in doing so, it helps to isolate economies away from

[2]Some authors like Rodrik (1994) have been able to explain that much of the growth rate in per capita income—between 53 and 67 percent, as opposed to 48 % for the World Bank estimated during the period 1960–1993, including also a Gini coefficient, measure for the degree of inequality in land distribution as a proxy for wealth distribution.

financial and economic crises. Obviously, in the domestic credit, as more loanable funds are canalized into the economy, the bigger economic growth is expected, whereas the lower the Interest rate spread, the greater its impact on growth will be.

The above results are shown in Table 4. The differences in growth experienced by the economies in the sample hinge on how well they manage income distribution to generate the right incentives among their economic agents, likewise, to induce the banking credit mostly into agricultural and industry activities, but also of the degree of financial integration they hold when the crash arose.

4 Economic Policy

According to the Gini coefficient, the more unequal countries—except Colombia have tended to reduce inequality after the 2008 financial crisis. This has been confirmed by Ostry et al. (2014) in his work for the IMF, which also added that countries with lower levels of inequality have a faster and more durable growth at a given level of redistribution, and that this redistribution, in general, has had a positive impact on economic growth.

Meanwhile, OECD (2012) states that three quarters of the reduction of economic inequality in Latin America is through transfers, the rest from taxes to the families. After taxes and transfers, as measured by the Gini index, income inequality is reduced by about 25 % at the end of the 2000s (OECD 2012); the most unequal countries tend to better redistribute. There is talk of pensions, unemployment insurance, child benefits, personal income taxes tending to be progressive, but consumption taxes and to property are the main tax entrants to the states. Some reforms on taxes and transfers have reduced inequality and increased the GDP per capita.

Meanwhile, other authors like Benabou (2000), Saint-Paul and Vertier (1993) suggest that progressive taxes have to be channeled into public investment, social benefits (education, health), or for the removal of market imperfections, which will improve the income distribution, and not only that, be beneficial for social development and economic growth.

5 Conclusion

A better income distribution by mean of taxes and targeted economic support, besides being beneficial for growth, it implies an improvement in the population's quality of life. The economic policy of each government should have this objective within their targets. On the other hand, a domestic financial system that can provide large loans, coupled with low differential interest rates, is a necessary condition for growth and proper functioning of the economy.

References

Benabou R (2000) Unequal societies: income distribution and the social contract. Am Econ Rev 90(1):96–129

Ostry MJD, Berg MA, Tsangarides MCG (2014) Redistribution, inequality, and growth Febrero SDN/14/02 Fondo Monetario Internacional

OECD (2012) Income inequality and growth: the role of taxes and transfers, OECD Economics Department Policy Notes, No. 9. Jan 2012

Rodrik D (1994) King Kong meets godzilla: the world bank and the East-Asian miracle. In: Fishlow A et al (eds) Miracle or design?: lessons from the East-Asian experience. ODC, Washington, D.C

Saint-Paul G, Verdier T (1993) Education, democracy and growth. J Dev Econ 42(2):399–407

Economic, Ecological, and Social Valuing of the *Cuniculus paca* Under the Ecuadorian Model of Good Living ("*Buen vivir*")

Elvira Rodriguez-Rios and Benjamin Garcia-Paez

Abstract Departing from the current development and Ecuadorian strategy, this paper assesses the wildlife species named *Cuniculus paca* as a source of bushmeat for local rural communities settled along the Pacific coast. At the outset, two premises are setup: on the one hand, a distinction is made between *Cuniculus paca* as a positional good and as a relational good and, on the other hand, custom is assumed lying behind in its chasing process. Thereby, it proposes a methodology to value the aforementioned specie from both economic and ecological standpoints, but also incorporating in the later, the variable Good Living ("*Buen vivir*"), which is measured by the level of satisfaction of the relational good that is coproduced along hunting. It is also assumed that this supplementary activity carried out by local people is largely a tradition passed on from one generation to another. The paper also calculates the abundance average relative index to place the *Cuniculus paca* population in the wild. An econometric model is then specified to estimate the effect of Good Living ("*Buen vivir*") on its social value of the *Cuniculus paca*. Based upon the estimated results, some right policies to ensure a sustainable management of such resource are brought to the fore to ensure the bushmeat consumption among local peasants, in line with the Good Living ("*Buen vivir*") convocation.

Keywords Economic value · Cultural value · Ecological value · Good living or "*Buen vivir*" · *Cuniculus paca* · Public policy

E. Rodriguez-Rios (✉)
Central Department of Research, Universidad Laica Eloy Alfaro de Manabí, Manta, Ecuador
e-mail: erodriguezrios.2011@gmail.com

B. Garcia-Paez
Department of Economics, DGAPA-Universidad Nacional Autónoma de México, Ciudad Universitaria, UNAM, 04315 Coyoacan, México DFMéxico DF
e-mail: garpaez@unam.mx

S. Soh (ed.), *Selected Papers from the Asia Conference on Economics & Business Research 2015*, DOI 10.1007/978-981-10-0986-0_11

1 Introduction

Hunting and consuming cynegetic species is a common practice of the forest-dwelling people both in tropical and neotropical areas worldwide. The bushmeat consumption has been broadly documented in the literature specialized (Golden et al. 2014; Rentsch and Damon 2013; Gardner and Davies 2013; Morra et al. 2009; Albrechtsen et al. 2006; de Merode et al. 2003). In Latin America, the use of wildlife in general and mammals in particular spreads over the region. One of the favorite mammals is the *Cuniculus paca*, which is widely consumed from Mexico to Argentina. Gallina et al. (2012) state that in Lacandon Jungle, Chiapas, Mexico, the 80 % of those households interviewed capture *Cuniculus paca* for food and Naranjo et al. (2004) demonstrated that in the Lacandon Jungle, Chiapas, Mexico, the annual extraction of biomass from species reached 8160 kg with higher rates of extraction corresponding to the *Cuniculus paca*. Its attractiveness not only obeys being a complementary protein source of rural local population (Aquino et al. 2009), but also its major role fulfilled in the ecosystem (Robinson and Redford 1991; Santos-Fita et al. 2012).

In Ecuador, according to the Wildlife Conservation Society (2010), 85 % of bushmeat sold in the Pompeya's market in the Eastern jungle of Ecuador is explained for mammals, such as *Cuniculus paca* but some parts of the Ecuadorian Amazon, the animal protein demand is satisfied at 100 % through hunting (Robinson and Redford 1991). The relevance of bushmeat in Ecuador is revealed by studies that analyze hunting relationships and others factors that influence the hunter's behaviour in the Ecuadorian Amazon (Sirén et al. 2006; De la Montaña et al. 2015); and the assessment of the sustainability of hunting in various indigenous communities in Ecuadorian Amazon (Zapata-Ríos et al. 2009).

In this view, this study aims to evaluate *Cuniculus paca* by implementing a methodology which combines economical, ecological, and social aspects so as to provide tangible elements to the Good Living model. Hence, our working hypothesis states that the socialeconomic value is an efficient way of valuing wildlife species like *Cuniculus paca* if we are determined to go beyond theoretical tenets invoked by the model of Good Living and thus to setup the right policies to manage it.

The *Cuniculus paca* is identified by local hunters themselves as their preferred pick among others surrounding wildlife species because of the tasteful meat provided. Its hunting is carried out by night when moon illumination level is low (Martins et al. 2007; Harmsen et al. 2011). In addition to its delicious meat, it plays a fundamental role in the neotropical ecosystems for its key position in the food chain, allowing the presence of species at higher levels and moreover for its important role as a seeds spreader, which ensures the survival of some plant species (Eisenberg and Redford 1999). As is easily grasped, the services delivered by *Cuniculus paca*, like that of any other wildlife species, do not get across formal markets so they do not have an explicit price as happening in the case of conventional goods and services.

Before starting analysis, it is necessary to grasp the essence of the Ecuadorian model of Good Living ("*Buen vivir*"). This development model was instituted in 2008 with the approval of Ecuador's new constitution. From this, the Good Living is translated into regulatory principles and is constituted with a guaranteed transverse axis by the development scheme (Constitution 2008, Chap. VI, art. 275) through countless declared constitutional rights (Title II, Chap. II). Theoretically, this new paradigm should be able to achieve both the Good Living of people and economic development. It demands a comprehensive vision of a multidimensional development system, which highlights an economic, social, and welfare system and a regime of Good Living, which happens to be a combination of equity and economic systems and social inclusion, in addition to the recognition of constitutional rights granted to nature.

The Good Living ("*Buen vivir*") is a community-based paradigm that the life is supported in the complementarity, reciprocity, and relationally. It considers the nature as an ecosystem of life. Under this biocentrism perspective, the Ecuadorian Good Living postulates the frugal use of nature, without opulence and without accumulation (Gudynas 2009).

The Good Living also holds in a solidary social and economic system (Constitution 2008, Chap. VII, Section I, art. 283) consisting of a mixed economy that includes as forms of public economic organization and private business like popular and solidary economies. The private economics is concerned about the balance market, on the contrary, the public economy one in conjunction looks for a popular economy both social and political equilibrium as well as the ecological, and it is achieved with self-organized labor according to the expanded reproduction of everyone's lives, where the real saver is the nature (Coraggio 2009).

According the Ecuadorian Good Living ("*Buen vivir*") development level is determined by either the income or consumption of the people as their satisfaction with life. The satisfaction level is measured as the amount of time devoted for relationship with other people (friends, the sons, and the family). It also considers the time dedicated to contemplation to nature (SENPLADES 2011). This demands to consider the right to the relationship with nature (Huanacuni Mamani 2010), which is recovered as a life principle that is recognized by Social Solidarity Economy in coexistence with the right to the property and the market.

2 Materials and Methods

2.1 Location of the Study Area

Flavio Alfaro is located in the northwest part of Manabí province, Ecuador (see Fig. 1). It encompasses 1343.1 km^2 and the surrounding areas of the Carmen y Chone, it occupies 156.9 km^2. The population is 37,422 inhabitants according to 2010 (National Institute of Statistics and Censuses 2011), distributed 51.8 % male and 48.2 % female, 16.6 % urban and 83.4 % of the population is rural.

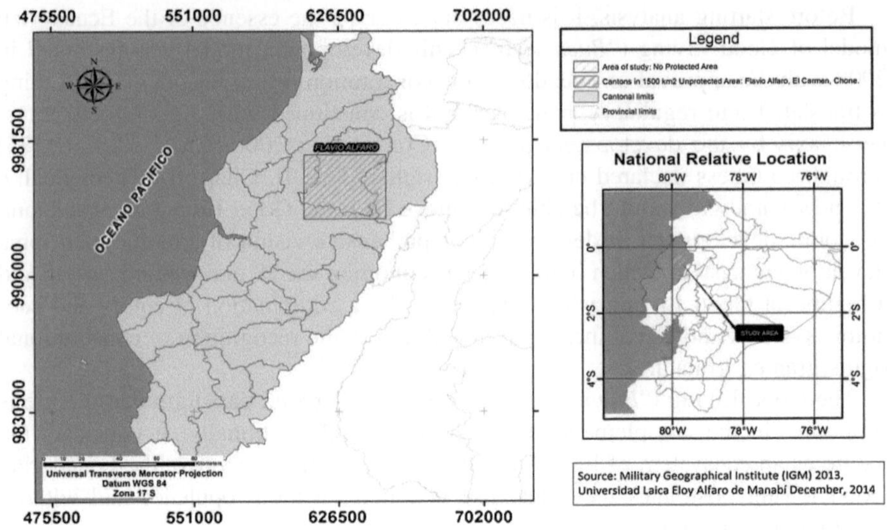

Fig. 1 Location of the study area

Almost all the study area is embraced by vegetation of tropical dry forest and very dry tropical forest that is not a protected area. It is located between the coordinates: Northwest Point: 00°17′03″ S and 80°01′24″ W. Northeast Point: 00°17′03″ S and 79°38′31″ W. South West Point: 00°26′45″ S and 80°01′24″ W. Southeast Point: 00°26′45″ S and 79°38′31″ W. It is an area characterized by the presence of coastal mountain ranges that reach an altitude between 350 and 500 m above sea level and with coastal valleys. The rainy season lasts from January to May and it drizzles in the dry season from June to December. Annual rainfall in this area ranges from 1000 to 2000 mm; the temperature varies between 22 and 26 °C. The core economic activities in Flavio Alfaro are agriculture, livestock, and forestry; so they make up the principal sources of earnings (Decentralized Autonomous Municipal Government Flavio Alfaro 2011). As aforementioned, subsistence hunting is a complementary activity; it is a legal activity under current Ecuadorian legislation. However, economic or social regulation is weak at its best.

2.2 *Data Collection and Empirical Analysis*

Raw data was collected by a socioeconomic survey conducted in February 2014 in the middle of the rainy season and having a statistical sample of 806 households. At one first stage, the units selected are those included in censuses sectors, which are the primary sampling units (United Nations 2005) constructed from enumeration areas identified and used in seventh national population census and sixth housing census 2010 in Ecuador (National Institute of Statistics and Censuses 2011),

Table 1 Variable description and expected sign

Variable	Notation	Description	Expected sign	Unit of value	Source
Social economic value	Sev	Social benefit obtained by Pev correction pondering it with the ecological factor, the factor of relational goods and the cultural factor. This is calculated: private economic value minus the discount rate for utilization for wildlife (from price the hunting license in Nuevo Leon state, Mexico. It is obtained S/.481 Mexican pesos in 2013 exchange rate US$ 1 = S/.13.14)	Positive	US$	Household survey
Private economic value	Pev	Private economic value or hunter profit [(Pq) − (IOC, rf, inp)]: gross income (price times quantity) minus three types of cost (opportunity cost personal income, fixed capital costs and other inputs, respectively)]. Pev is realized in the bushmeat consumption process by the hunters and their families	Positive	US$	Household survey
Good Living or "*Buen vivir*"	Bv	It is structured from three factors of Good Living ("*Buen vivir*"): relative abundance of game species (Ra), relational goods (Rg) and the cultural factor (Cu). This variable "*Buen vivir*" is an index that we obtain by the following formula: [1 + ((Ra + Cu + Rg)/3)]	Positive	Index	Calculus
Relative abundance	Ra	The relative *Cuniculus paca* abundance index [based on estimates obtained according to the methodology proposed by Beck-King and Von Helversen (1999)]	Positive	Index	Calculus
Relational Good	Rg	The relational Good produced at the hunting process which by the hunter is related to nature in the act of hunting	Positive	0–1	Household survey
Custom	Cu	The ancestral custom of hunting for subsistence that comes from years ago	Positive	0–1	Household survey

whereas in a second stage the houses are chosen to comply with the stylised facts put forward by the same census: first, over 95 % of the population living in the study area, there is a single household living in National Institute of Statistics and

Censuses (2011), and secondly that such kind of housing unit is a stable living place and easily identifiable in the area rural. Hence, the distribution of second stage units were determined from numbers of houses (it is assumed each house is ruled by a household) in the Primary Sample Units based on the seventh population census Ecuador (National Institute of Statistics and Censuses 2011).

The variables used in the regression model are described as follows (see Table 1).

In the valuing process of the *Cuniculus paca,* we recur to the method of indirect opportunity cost of labor (IOC) to value, in monetary terms, the time devoted properly to the ritual of stalking implied but also including the assigned time to go back and forth the forest. The cost of hunting tools and instruments (fc) is transferred to the bushmeat by linear depreciation over their useful life established in five years and the cost of ammunitions and cost of food and drink (inp) used for hunting are valued at market retail price.

Bushmeat production (q) and price (P) variables result from observation. The fixed capital (fc), labor cost (IOC) variable, supplies (inp), total cost (TC), and income (I) variables were constructed from observed variables such as: invested time in hunting events in the period of study, amount and types of inputs, and the number and type of hunting tools and instruments, and so on. This input is used to construct the vector of the variable private economic value (Pev). Furthermore, secondary sources of information were used: unified monthly wage in Ecuador legislated in 2013 (US$318), retail market price of inputs and tools and instruments, and International Accounting Standards (IASs). It should be noted that along with socioeconomic information provided by the household survey, the data available on the relative abundance (Ra) of the species *Cuniculus paca* were analyzed too.

3 Valuing of the *Cuniculus paca*

The Sev is the net benefit accrued by society from the consumption of the *Cuniculus paca* meat. Hence, this Sev is a function of the private economic value and the externalities measured by the index of Good Living ("*Buen vivir*"). This index was constructed based upon the relative *Cuniculus paca* abundance, the relational good produced at the hunting time, and custom of the ancestral practicing of hunting for subsistence reasons. So, social economic value is expressed as follows:

$$\text{Sev} = f\,(\text{Pev, Ra, Rg, Cu}) \tag{1}$$

To obtain Sev a log-linear model is specified in the grounds proposed by Rodriguez-Rios (2015):

$$\ln \text{Sev} = \delta_1 \text{Pev} + \delta_2 \text{Bv}_i + \varepsilon_i \tag{2}$$

where: Sev = Social economic value, Pev = Private economic value and Bv = the *dummy* variable "*Buen vivir*". $\delta_1, \ldots, \delta_2$ are parameters to be estimated.

The model specification (2) is based on positive economic theory and empirical evidence on hunting of the *Cuniculus paca*. This is a single-equation model that has been estimated by ordinary least squares (OLS) in Stata v13, based on 43 observations.

4 Results and Conclusions

The overall estimation procedure of the social economic value of *Cuniculus paca* goes through two broad stages. The first one defines each of the factors of the Good Living ("*Buen vivir*"): Relative abundance of the *Cuniculus paca* local population (Ra), the relational good (Rg), and the cultural factor (Cu), while in the second stage the regression equation specified (2) is estimated.

Being a key variable the Good Living ("*Buen vivir*"), it is worthy to say that the relative abundance (Ra) of the *Cuniculus paca* in Flavio Alfaro and neighboring villages is calculated in 0.3 *Paca* number per hectare or 30 individual per km^2. This index is an average of the abundance relative of the *Cuniculus paca* of 30 sampled sites in the study area (Eloy Alfaro University technical report 2014), using methodology by Beck-King and Von Helversen (1999). As a whole, the sub-variables above mentioned become a sort of a benchmark to calculate the index Good Living ("*Buen vivir*"), using the formula specified above (Table 1) and the following scaling (Table 2).

After estimation, the results obtained are as follow:

$$\begin{aligned} \ln \text{Sev} &= 2.873 + 0.0054\,\text{Pev} + 0.906\,\text{Bv} \\ \text{s.e.}: &\qquad (0.193) \quad (0.00109) \quad (0.183) \end{aligned}$$

Table 2 Good Living (Bv) variable classification

Good Living ("*Buen vivir*") Factors[a]	Good Living ("*Buen vivir*") Index	*Dummy* Good Living ("*Buen vivir*") (Bv)[b]
It fulfills all factors of the good living (Rg, Cu *y* Ra)	1.75	1
It fulfills at least with two of the factors of the good living	1.42	0
It fulfills at least with one factor of the good living	1.08	0

Notes
[a]The Good Living ("*Buen vivir*") factors: Ra, Rg, Cu
[b]*Buen vivir* (Bv) categorical variable

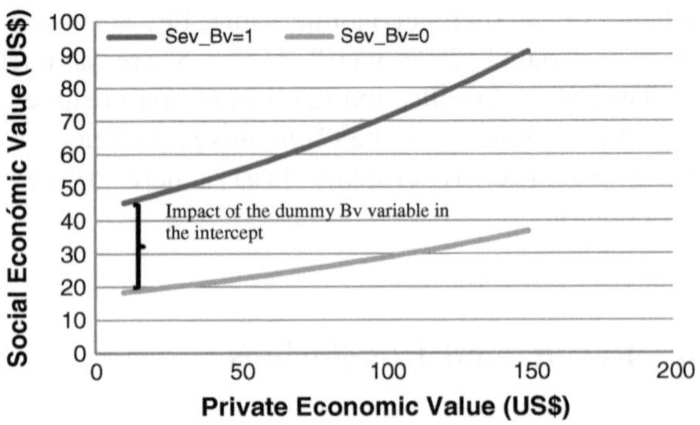

Fig. 2 The effect of variable "*Buen vivir*" (Bv) on the social economic value (Sev)

Estimate findings show that the coefficients linked to the regressor variables Pev and Bv representing the good life are statistically significant at 0.05 level. Overall significance of the model is acceptable ($F_{(2,40)} = 38.78$; $p = 0.000$). The private economic value and Good Living ("*Buen vivir*") explains, on average, 79.2 % of variation in the Sev of the *Cuniculus paca* ($R^2 = 0.792$). The results also show that throughout the hunting period in 2013, when the Pev increased in one dollar, *ceteris paribus,* the Sev grows 0.54 %. The impact of the "*Buen vivir*" variable on the Sev is 90.6 %. This situation corresponds when hunters show a higher level of satisfaction by the effect of the index of relative abundance of *Cuniculus paca*, the cultural factor and the satisfaction that hunters had felt when they were hunting in the forest. The magnitude of the impact of variable Bv, 0.91 explains the difference between the social average value of households that hunted the *Cuniculus paca* and those who did not. The impact of the Bv variable is illustrated in Fig. 2.

In a nutshell, (a) the main motivation for *Cuniculus paca's* hunting and consumption is the custom of tasting by the exquisite flavor of its meat, (b) In accordance to 2013 data, monthly consumption of *Cunniculus paca* ranks fifth (1.6 %) after the chicken meat (32.7 %), the fish meat (31.3 %), the pork (20.5 %), and beef (13.4 %) (Rodriguez-Rios 2015). Undoubtedly, the consumption of bushmeat not only *Cuniculus paca*, but also other species such as agouti (*Dasyprocta Punctata*), nine-banded armadillo (*Dasypus Novemcinctus*), Peccary (*Pecari Tajacu*), among others is a relevant issue as it is a factor that supports the achievement of Good Living ("*Buen vivir*") of the inhabitants of rural local communities in the Ecuadorian coast that in the case of Ecuador is a challenge seen from the need to achieve the earthly realm of Good Living ("*Buen vivir*") and, (c) in the short term, the opportunity cost for rural people in the process of stepping in a more sustainable hunting is not so high (Bodmer and Lozano 2001).

The findings also indicate that meat of wild *Cuniculus paca* plays a small relative role in household earnings in comparison to the spiritual gain obtained by local inhabitants.[1]

[1]In fact, the sale of *Cuniculus paca* meat contributes only 5 % of the overall household budget surveyed (Rodriguez-Rios 2015).

5 Discussion and Policy Options

Although the consumption of meat of wild species *Cuniculus paca* is a vital part of the diet of dwelling households in the study area, the research results drawn suggest that underlying hunting motivations such as incidence of its relative abundance index, its relational value and the custom to consume bushmeat, as a whole, weight the own hunter's decision of hunting it. In other words, not only technical factors intervene in such a decision. In this view, public policy for a sustainable use management must include the following strategic elements:

(1) Given that the social appreciation of wildlife stocks includes the enjoyment of property and relational expression using species like the *Cuniculus paca* in a sustainable manner and custom, this assessment proposal should be taken as a benchmark for making public policy to ensure the dual objective: achieving a degree of Good Living ("*Buen vivir*") of communities while natural endowment is preserved.
(2) Inducement of extraction levels of *Cuniculus paca* is compatible to that the suggested social value amount of US$ 4451.51 in the hunting period 2013 (the coefficients estimated for each independent variable was used to predict economic, ecological and social value of *Cuniculus paca*).
(3) Promote the organization of hunters into communities capable of interpreting the new relationship between nature and humans proposed by the "*Buen vivir*" paradigm as a means to ensure natural reproduction of the species as attempts to "overcome the fence built by the anthropocentrism characteristic of Modernity" (Gudynas 2010a, p. 47). It will dedicate to sustainable management, the hunting subsistence to ensure the self-consumption the bushmeat of the local households.
(4) Recognition of the fact that hunters are basically motivated by social benefits associated with *Cuniculus paca* and others cynegetic species rather than purely economic motives may assist in making of appropriate local management. As shown, the 97.8 % of total households surveyed declares to devote the bushmeat produced to self-consumption and only the remaining, 2.2 %, is for sale (Rodriguez-Rios 2015).
(5) Explicitly admit that efficient economic and noneconomic mechanisms to regulate the consumption of bushmeat are needed to address many other aspects, implications, and relevant relationships which, in turn, require further analysis and specific studies, for instance: future research emphasizing deforestation as a major factor in the decline of populations of species of wildlife; studies analyzing the nutritional, cultural, and gastronomic importance of the *Cuniculus paca* and related close species. Research to determine the stock of the species in the wild and on the various ecosystem services.

Furthermore, our empirical findings support the results obtained by Gallina et al. (2012) who assessed the consumption of *Cunniculus paca* at the Sierra-de-Tabasco State Park in Mexico in the same line than us, and also those gathered by Valsecchi et al. (2014) in the ingestion of such wild species but in Brazil. Likewise, Altrichter and Almeida (2002) demonstrated that *Cuniculus paca* is the main species consumed in 15 communities on the Osa Peninsula, Costa Rica. Also our results are related with the conclusions of Sirén (2012) that focus in the consumption bushmeat in the communities of the Ecuadorian Amazon.

Our proposals for public policy action look for the addition of a set of social policies of Good Living ("*Buen vivir*") designed and based on the development of human capabilities (Sen 1999) to "*Buen vivir*" of forest-dwelling peoples.

The evaluation of the *Cuniculus paca* considered the abundance relative this cynegetic specie in an attempt combining ecological and social aspects with economic valuation of wild *Cuniculus paca* (Admiraal et al. 2013; Costanza et al. 2015). The economic evaluation is only one dimension of the overall value of nature that is indicated Turner (1999). Hence, it would not be adequate if it is not taken into account other dimensions of the value embodying fully ecosystem sustainability (Admiraal et al. 2013). Also, Gudynas (2010b) indicates that the environment must be assessed through other methods besides economic, considering others values as cultural, social, and ecological. However, methods as contingent valuation have been used widely to environmental evaluation. There is a set of studies over the economic valuing of natural resources both marketed and non-marketed that have used this method the valuation contingent (Piran-White et al. 1997; Loomis and White 1996; Tietenberg and Lynne 2015; Gelo and Koch 2015), and others such as the travel cost method (Badola et al. 2010), Hedonic Property Values and so on.

Our method combines both the tangible good (hunted prey) and the non-material hunter's consumption (Kasser 2003) in accordance with the Ecuadorian model for the Good Living ("*Buen vivir*"). Therefore, we included not only the monetary costs and benefits, but also include the nonmarketed contribution as the human–nature relations, which give satisfaction felt by the hunter. It is part of an integrative definition of well-being and quality of life (Costanza et al. 2015). Estimating the contribution of these two goods on the Good Living ("*Buen vivir*") of the local population is the major advantage of our methodological approach. Moreover, the results agree with similar studies and can be applied to other close cynegetic species.

References

Admiraal JF, Wossink A, de Groot More W, de Snoo GR (2013) More than total economic value: How to combine economic valuation of biodiversity with ecological resilience. Ecol Econ 89:115–122

Albrechtsen L, Fa J, Barry B, McDonald D (2006) Contrasts in availability and consumption of animal protein in Bioko Island, West Africa: the role of bushmeat. Environ Conserv 32(4): 340–348

Altrichter M, Almeida R (2002) Explotation of whitelipped peccaries Tayassu pecari (Artiodactyla: Tayassuidae) on the Osa Peninsula, Costa Rica. Oryx 36(2):126–132

Aquino R, Gil D, Pezo E (2009) Aspectos ecológicos y sostenibilidad de la caza del majás (Cuniculus paca) en la cuenca del rio Itaya, Amazonia peruana. Rev Peruana Biol 16(1):67–72

Badola R, Hussain SA, Mishra BK, Konthoujam B, Thapliyal S, Dhakate PM (2010) Assessment of ecosystem services of Corbett Tiger Reserve, India. Environmentalist 30:320–329

Beck-King H, Von Helversen O (1999) Home range, population density, and food resources of Agouti paca (Rodentia: Agoutidae) in Costa Rica: a study using alternative methods. Biotropica 31(4):675–685

Bodmer RE, Lozano PE (2001) Rural development and sustainable wildlife use in Peru. Conserv Biol 15(4):1163–1170

Constitution of the Republic of Ecuador (2008) Registro Oficial, 449, October 20, 2008

Coraggio J (2009) Economía del Trabajo. www.coraggioeconomia.org/jlc/.../Economia_Del_Trabajo_2009.doc

Costanza R, Cumberland JH, Herman D, Goodland R, Norgaard RB, Kubiszewski I, Franco C (2015) An introduction to ecological economics, 2nd edn. CRC Press

Decentralized Autonomous Municipal Government Flavio Alfaro (2011) Plan de Desarrollo y Ordenamiento Territorial. http://app.sni.gob.ec/sni-link/sni/%23recycle/PDyOTs%202014/1360002840001/PDyOT/18022013_150736_FLAVIO%20ALFARO.pdf

De la Montaña E, Moreno-Sánchez R, Maldonado J, Griffith D (2015) Predicting hunter behavior of indigenous communities in the Ecuadorian Amazon: insights from a household production model. Ecol Soc (in press)

de Merode E, Homewood K, Cowlishaw G (2003) The value of bushmeat and other wild foods to rural households living in extreme poverty in Democratic Republic of Congo. Biol Conserv 118:573–581

Eisenberg JF, Redford KH (1999) Mammals of the Neotropics: the Central Neotropics, vol. 3, 1st edn. The University of Chicago Press, Ecuador, Peru, Bolivia, Brazil

Eloy Alfaro University of Manabí (2014) Research project: "Sostenibilidad de la cacería y otros aspectos ecológicos de la guanta (*Cuniculus paca*) y de otras especies cinegéticas importantes en un paisaje antropogénico y en un área protegida de la provincia de Manabí". Technical report. Manta. Griffith D

Gallina S, Pérez-Torres J, Guzmán-Aguirre C (2012) Use of the paca, Cuniculus paca (Rodentia: Agoutidae) in the Sierra de Tabasco State Park, Mexico. Biol Trop 60(3):1345–1355

Gardner C, Davies ZG (2013) Rural bushmeat consumption whithin multiple-use protected areas: qualitative evidence from Southwest Madagascar. Hum Ecol. doi:10.1007/s10745-013-9629-1

Gelo D, Koch SF (2015) Contingent valuation of community forestry programs in Ethiopia: controlling for preference anomalies in double-bounded CVM

Golden CD, Bonds MH, Brashares JS, Rodolph Rasolofoniaina BJ, Kremen C (2014) Economic valuation of subsistence harvest of wildlife in Madagascar. Conserv Biol 28(1):234–243

Gudynas E (2009) La dimensión ecológica del buen vivir: entre el fantasma de la modernidad y el desafío biocéntrico. OBETS: Rev Cienc Soc 4:49–53

Gudynas E (2010a) The biocentric path: intrinsic values, Nature rights and ecological justice. Tabula Rasa 13:45–71 (Colombia)

Gudynas E (2010b) Desarrollo sostenible: una guía básica de conceptos y tendencias hacia otra economía. Otra Econ 4(6):42–66

Harmsen B, Foster R, Silver S, Ostro L, Doncaster C (2011) Jaguar and puma activity patterns in relation to their main prey. Mamm Biol 76:320–324

Huanacuni Mamani F (2010) Buen vivir/Vivir Bien. Filosofía, políticas, estrategias y experiencias regionales andinas. Coordinadora Andina de Organizaciones Indígenas (CAOI). Lima, Perú

Kasser T (2003) The high price of materialism. The MIT Press, Cambridge, MA

Loomis JB, White DS (1996) Economic benefits of rare and endangered species: summary and meta-analysis. Ecol Econ 18:197–206

Martins SS, Sanderson JG, Silva JS (2007) Monitoring mammals in the Caxiuanã National Forest, Brazil—first results from the Tropical Ecology, Assessment and Monitoring (TEAM) program. Biodivers Conserv 16(4):857–870

Morra W, Gail H, Buck AJ (2009) The market for bushmeat: Colobus satanas on Bioko Island. Ecol Econ 68:2619–2626
Naranjo E, Guerra M, Bodmer RE, Bolaños JE (2004) Subsistence hunting by three ethnic groups of the Lacandon Forest, Mexico. J Ethnobiol 24:233–253
National Institute of Statistics and Censuses of Ecuador (2011) VII censo de población y VI censo de vivienda. www.inec.gob.ec
Piran-White CL, Keith GW, Patrick LJ, Richards G (1997) Economic values of threatened mammals in Britain: a case study of the otter *lutra lutra* and the water vole *Arvicola terrestris*. Biol Conserv 82:345–354
Rodriguez-Rios EB (2015) Economic, ecological and social valuing of the hunting species food providers for rural communities. The case of the Cuniculus paca in Flavio Alfaro, Manabí, Ecuador. Ph.D. thesis, Mexico UNAM University, Mexico DF, p 182
Rentsch D, Damon A (2013) Prices, poaching, and protein alternatives: an analysis of bushmeat consumption around Serengeti National Park, Tanzania. Ecol Econ 91:1–9
Robinson JG, Redford KH (1991) Sustainable harvest of neotropical forest animals. In: Robinson JG, Redford KH (eds) Neotropical wildlife use and conservation. The University of Chicago Press, Chicago, pp 415–429
Santos-Fita D, Naranjo E, Rangel-Salazar J (2012) Wildlife uses and hunting patterns in rural communities of the Yucatan Peninsula, Mexico. J Ethnobiol Ethnomed 8:38
Sen A (1999) Development as freedom. Anchor, New York, USA
SENPLADES, Secretaria Nacional de Planificación y Desarrollo (2011) La felicidad como medida del Buen vivir en el Ecuador. SENPLADES, Quito-Ecuador
Sirén AH, Cardenas JC, Machoa JD (2006) The relation between income and hunting in tropical forests: an economic experiment in the field. Ecol Soc 11(1):44
Sirén AH (2012) Festival hunting by the kichwa people in the Ecuadorean Amazon. J Ethnobiol 32(1):30–50
Tietenberg T, Lynne L (2015) Environmental & natural resource economics, 10th edn. Pearson, USA
Turner RK (1999) The place of economic values in environmental valuation. In: Bateman IJ, Willis KG (eds) Valuing environmental preferences: theory and practice of the contingent valuation method in the US, EU, and developing Countries. Oxford University Press, Oxford, pp 17–41
United Nations (2005) Household sample surveys in developing and transition countries, New York
Valsecchi J, El Bizri HR, Figueira JEC (2014) Subsistence hunting of Cuniculus paca in the middle of the Solimões River Amazonas, Brazil. J Biol 74(3):560–568
Wildlife Conservation Society WCS (2010) The global conservation program achievements and lessons learned from 10 years of support for threats-based conservation at a landscape and seascape scale. Greater Yasuní-Napo Moist Forest landscape conservation area (Ecuador). http://pdf.usaid.gov/pdf_docs/Pdacp728.pdf
Zapata-Ríos G, Urgilés C, Suárez E (2009) Mammal hunting by the Shuar of the Ecuadorian Amazon: is it sustainable? Oryx 43:375–385

The Relationship Between Organizational Dynamics and Total Quality Management Practices of Manufacturing and Other Related Companies in the CALABARZON Region, Philippines

Rogel L. Limpiada

Abstract The organizational dynamics serves as fuel to implement various programs in a company. Pursuing the implementation of programs like Total Quality Management (TQM) would require effective and efficient dynamics in the organization. This study was conducted to determine the correlation between organizational dynamics and TQM practices of the manufacturing companies and other related businesses in Region 4A-CALABARZON. A total of 109 employees of these companies served as respondents of the study. It was found that these respondents are typically representing the manufacturing sector, with companies which initiated customer satisfaction initiatives, were ISO14001 certified, and have received quality management excellence award. In terms of organizational dynamics, the study found out that the companies are performing well in the areas of purpose, management, leadership, attitude toward change, and relationships. Moreover, organizational dynamics are significantly correlated with TQM practices. In the end, the study recommends that the companies surveyed should continuously strive to further enhance dynamism in terms of rewards, governance, structures, and resources.

Keywords Organizational dynamics · Total Quality Management · Practices

R.L. Limpiada (✉)
Royal Institute of Educators, Royal Institution, Singapore, Singapore
e-mail: rlimpiada@yahoo.com

R.L. Limpiada
College of Education, Institute of Graduate Studies and Research, Manuel S. Enverga University Foundation, Lucena City, Philippines

S. Soh (ed.), *Selected Papers from the Asia Conference on Economics & Business Research 2015*, DOI 10.1007/978-981-10-0986-0_12

1 Literature Review

1.1 Total Quality Management Practices

Several studies had been conducted to illuminate concepts and ideas about Total Quality Management (TQM). TQM according to BS7850: Part 1 (1992) is a management philosophy and company practices that aim to harness the human material resources from an organization in the most effective way to achieve the objectives of the organization. Likewise, BS 4778: Part 2 (1991) considers TQM as a management philosophy embracing all activities through which the needs and expectations of the customer and the community, and the objectives of the organization are satisfied in the most efficient and cost effective way by maximizing the potential of all employees in a continuing drive for improvement. TQM had its earlier development with Deming (1986) who postulated a major philosophy in quality improvement through statistical control and reduction of variability. Juran (1988) shared his definition of quality as "fitness for use" which attained widespread although not universal acceptance. He further theorized on the quality trilogy: quality planning, quality control, and quality improvement. In 1980, Crosby conceptualized zero defects. This is the attitude of defect prevention and involves doing the "right job right the first time." Quality according to Crosby (1984) is free, but it is not a gift. Feigenbaum (1991) emphasizes total quality control. According to him, a company must set quality standards, appraise conformance to standards, act when conditions are not met, and plan to make improvements. Finally, Ishikawa (1985) advocated the use of statistical techniques to improve quality in Japanese industry and his greatest achievement was the successful introduction of Quality Control Circles into Japan.

1.2 The CALABARZON Region in the Philippines

CALABARZON is one of the regions of the Philippines. It is designated as Region IV-A and its regional center is Calamba City in Laguna. The region is composed of five provinces, namely: **Ca**vite, **La**guna, **Ba**tangas, **R**izal, and Que**zon**; whose names form the acronym CALABARZON. The region is also more formally known as Southern Tagalog Mainland. The region is in Southwestern Luzon, just south and east of Metro Manila and is the second most densely populated region. CALABARZON and MIMAROPA were previously together known as Southern Tagalog, until they were separated in 2002 by virtue of Executive Order No. 103. Executive Order No. 246, dated October 28, 2003, designated Calamba City as the regional center of CALABARZON. The largest city of the CALABARZON region and the second most highly urbanized city is Antipolo, with Lucena City being the first. CALABARZON is the most populated region in the Philippines, with a population of 12,609,803 inhabitants. CALABARZON is the second largest contributor to the national GDP, accounting for 17 % of the gross domestic product. The region boasts a 2.1 % inflation rate, lower than the national average of 3 %. The region has a 9.2 % unemployment rate which is higher than the national average of 7 %. CALABARZON, much like the rest of the country, is caught in the middle of being an industrial and an agricultural economy. Due to CALABARZON's proximity to Metro Manila, a large amount of urbanization has taken place over the years. Cavite and Laguna in particular are sites of manufacturing and high-tech industries, with companies like Intel and Panasonic setting up plants in the region. Santa Rosa, Laguna, is home to a host of semiconductor and automotive companies such as Amkor and Toyota, while Gen. Trias is home to Cavite's largest economic development zone, the PEC Industrial Park.

2 Research Methodology

2.1 Sampling Design

A total of 109 randomly selected respondents participated in the study. Majority of them are from manufacturing companies accounting to around 67.05 %. Other respondents were drawn from related industry or sectors like services.

2.2 Research Procedure

The World Bank Office Manila reported in its quarterly economic updates, released in December 2012 that manufacturing accounts for two-thirds of industrial output. It benefitted from a rebound in exports and grew 5.7 % in the third quarter. Knowing that the CALABARZON region is a host to a number of manufacturing companies located in various industrial parks of the region, the researcher thought of conducting a study on operations of these companies. The researcher decided to correlate TQM practices of the companies with their perceived impact on their operations. A questionnaire was designed based on the instrument used in the study entitled "Survey on the Implementation of Total Quality Management in Malaysian Automotive Suppliers" conducted by Univirsiti Teknologi Malaya. After the modification of the aforementioned instrument, the modified questionnaires were then distributed to targeted respondents. After which, the said instruments were retrieved. Responses were tallied using MS Excel and corresponding statistical tools were applied such as frequency and percentage, weighted means, and correlation analysis.

3 Data Analysis

Question 1. What is the typical profile of the respondents?
Figure 1 shows the typical profile of the respondents. As shown, the 109 respondents are typically employees of manufacturing companies accounting to 74 or 67.89 %. Their companies have initiated customer satisfaction initiatives as reported by 60 or 55.05 %. Certification to ISO 14001 was reported by 50 or 45.87 % of the respondents. Finally, forty-six or 42.20 % of the respondents have said that their companies received Quality Management award.

Question 2. What is the degree of agreement of the respondents on the indicators of their organizational dynamics?
Table 1 shows the weighted means of the degree of agreement of the respondents on their organizational dynamics along the nine indicators. The general weighted mean of 2.09 indicates that they slightly agree that the nine aspects of organizational dynamics are present in their companies. Of the nine aspects, they gave the

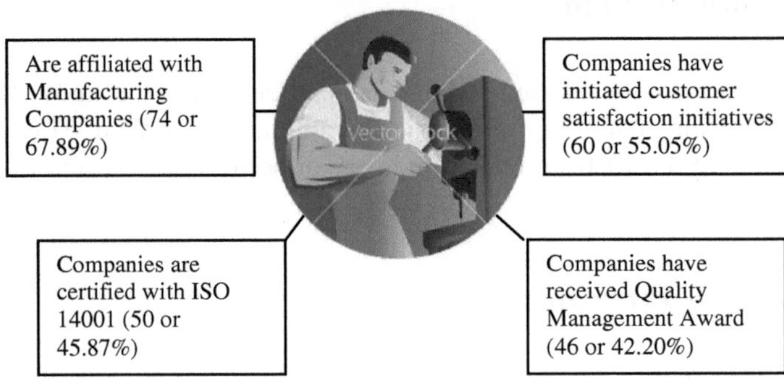

Fig. 1 Typical profile of the respondents

Table 1 Weighted means of the degree of agreement of the respondents on their organizational dynamics

	Aspects of organizational dynamics	Weighted mean	Verbal interpretation	Rank
1	Purpose	1.88	Slightly agree	1
2	Management	1.94	Slightly agree	2
3	Leadership	1.98	Slightly agree	3
4	Attitude toward change	2.00	Slightly agree	4
5	Relationships	2.08	Slightly agree	5
6	Rewards	2.12	Slightly agree	6
7	Governance	2.17	Slightly agree	7
8	Structures	2.23	Slightly agree	8
9	Resources	2.39	Slightly agree	9
	General weighted mean	2.09	Slightly agree	

Table 2 Weighted means of the assessment of the respondents on their Total Quality Management practices

	Aspects of Total Quality Management practices	Weighted mean	Verbal interpretation	Rank
1	Work environment and culture	4.25	Very good	1
2	Management leadership	4.16	Very good	2
3	Education and training	4.15	Very good	3
4	Supplier quality management	4.13	Very good	4
5	Systems and processes	4.12	Very good	5
6	Continuous improvement	4.09	Very good	6
7	Measurement and feedback	3.97	Very good	7
8	Resource management	3.84	Very good	8
	General weighted mean	4.09	Very good	

highest three ratings to purpose, management, and leadership. On the other hand, in the bottom three are governance, structures, and resources.

Question 3. What is the respondents assessment of their Total Quality Management practices?
Table 2 shows the assessment made by the respondents on their Total Quality Management practices. They have reported that their TQM practices along the nine aspects is very good as evident in the general weighted mean of 4.09. The top three raters are the TQM practices along with work environment and culture, management leadership, and education and training. In the bottom three are their practices on continuous improvement, measurement and feedback, and resource management.

Question 4. Is there any significant relationship between organizational dynamics and TQM practices of the companies in the CALABARZON region?
Table 3 shows the t-test results to determine if there exists a significant relationship between organizational dynamics and TQM practices of companies in the

Table 3 t-Test results to determine if there is a significant relationship between organizational dynamics and TQM practices

	Aspects of organizational dynamics correlated with TQM practices	t-stat	Conclusion
1	Purpose	37.07	Significantly correlated
2	Governance	35.36	Significantly correlated
3	Relationship	37.02	Significantly correlated
4	Structures	36.17	Significantly correlated
5	Management	36.39	Significantly correlated
6	Resources	36.01	Significantly correlated
7	Leadership	36.89	Significantly correlated
8	Rewards	36.61	Significantly correlated
9	Attitude towards change	37.73	Significantly correlated

t-critical: 1.98 @ 0.05 level of significance

CALABARZON region. The t-test results showed that the t-computed values are less than the t-critical value of 1.98. This means that the aspects of organizational dynamics such as purpose, governance, relationship, structures, management, resources, leadership, rewards, and attitude towards change are significantly correlated with TQM practices.

4 Conclusion and Discussion

It was theorized at the outset of the study that there could be a relationship between organizational dynamics and TQM practices of companies. This study concludes that based on the typical profile of the respondents, they have implemented TQM along with the prevailing organizational dynamics. It was found in the study that the companies have performed better in the areas of purpose, management, leadership, attitude towards change and relationships. These areas of organizational dynamics can also be regarded in the continuum of organizational culture. Findings on organizational dynamics are related to findings of previous studies like that of Grondahl and Martinsson (2011) where they have found out that the rational culture is supporting several quality practices, which have been used to bring suggestions on how the unit can continue to develop their quality management. They concluded that in order to achieve high performance in the process management practice, it is important to increase the feeling of empowerment among employees and to involve the people closest to the process. According to Lawal and Chukwuebuka (2007), it is necessary that leadership recognizes the needs of the workers, employ appropriate motivational tool such as promotion of staff based on merit skills, provide suitable working environment and provide appropriate leadership style that will encourage free flow of information among employer, superior officers and other employees. As a recommendation of this study, the companies need to focus more on rewards, governance, structures, and resources aspects. TQM practices that these companies were able to perform well include purpose, management, leadership, attitude toward change and relationships. On TQM practices, the findings would lead to the recommendation that the participants in the survey may focus more on further enhancing their practices along with rewards, governance, structure, and resources.

References

BS 4778: Part 2 (1991) Quality concepts related definitions. British Standards Institution, London

Crosby PB (1984) Quality is free: the art of making quality certain. New American Library, New York

Deming WE (1986) Out of the crisis. Masachusetts Institute of Technology Center for Advanced Engineering Study, Cambridge

Feigenbaum AV (1991) Total quality control, 3rd edn. McGraw-Hill Inc, New York

Grondahl E, Martinsson L (2011) Impact of organizational culture on quality management. Chalmers University of Technology

Ishikawa K (1985) What is Total quality control? The Japanese way (trans: Lu DJ). Prentice Hall, Englewood Cliffs
Juran JM (1988) The quality function. In: Juran's quality handbook, 4th edn, pp 2.7, 2.8
Lawal OY, Chukwuebuka CK (2007) Evaluation of leadership and organizational performance in small scale industries in Nigeria. In: A case of selected small scale industries in Aba. Aba State, Nigeria

Examining the Preferences of Online Business Course Students

Gary F. Keller

Abstract There were three purposes to this study; (a) ascertain why students chose to enroll in online courses and the number taken to date in their academic careers in the College of Business at a regional University, (b) determine the preferences of 300 and 400 level course participants regarding online interaction, feedback, and course design, and (c) find out participants' specific complaints about faculty members' practices and elicit recommendations for course design improvements. Results from the study indicated; (a) the average number of online courses taken by course participants was 8.5; (b) course participants: valued interaction with faculty, appreciated supplemental course materials (e.g., videos, web links, etc.), did not expect an online class to be similar to a face-to-face class, were nearly equally split regarding the value of graded discussions, valued simplicity of course design, content and amount of interaction in online courses, and did not value audio feedback on written assignments. Finally, replies to two qualitative questions regarding course improvements and things that aggravated online students indicated that, while there were statistically significant differences between 300 and 400 level participants' online course expectations both groups point to the need for faculty improvements in terms of course design and instructional methodology. Four recommendations were made for future research and implementation.

Keywords Online learning · Online course design · Student preferences for online business courses

G.F. Keller (✉)
College of Business, Eastern Oregon University, La Grande, OR 97850-2807, USA
e-mail: gkeller@eou.edu
URL: https://www.eou.edu

S. Soh (ed.), *Selected Papers from the Asia Conference on Economics & Business Research 2015*, DOI 10.1007/978-981-10-0986-0_13

1 Introduction

The availability of online course offerings by universities throughout the world continues to grow significantly. "The 2012 Survey of Online Learning reveals that the number of students taking at least one online course has now surpassed 6.7 million" (Online learning consortium 2012, para 1). Harvard University alone reported in July 2015 that it had 2,810,009 registrants for all HarvardX Offerings from 195 countries (Harvardx 2015). The near-universal adoption of online learning offerings by universities throughout the world has created a stimulating discussion regarding the design and functionality of internet-based courses. Some assert that online courses should be reproductions of the format and interactions of face-to-face classes. Others claim that due to the nature of online education frequently delivered in an achromous format, constrained by varying levels of internet connectivity and bandwidth capacity, hardware/software disparities, etc., online classes cannot replicate the appearance and composition of face-to-face courses. Numerous research studies in the literature discuss faculty preparation for teaching online courses, student penchants regarding grading of online assignments, class discussions, etc., online course content and design why students choose online courses and their recommendations for course delivery improvements.

There were three purposes to this study; (a) ascertain why students chose to enroll in online courses and how many courses they took to this point in their academic careers in the College of Business, (b) determine the preferences of 300 and 400 level course participants regarding online interaction, feedback, and course design, and (c) find out participants' specific complaints and suggested improvements about faculty members' practices and recommendations for course design improvements. A pre-course, mixed method survey instrument was used to gather data from 239 students enrolled in nine junior/senior level online business classes over four terms taught by the researcher in the College of Business at a regional university located in the Pacific Northwest of the United States of America. There were 175 valid responses for a participation rate of 73 %. Involvement was voluntary; the identities of respondents were anonymous.

2 Literature Review

The emphasis of the literature review was to find what students and faculty members consider as vital attributes for a successful online course. Sun and Ganesh (2014) reported on student reactions to an online MBA marketing research course. The researchers found that students enrolled in the online version of the course performed comparably to their face-to-face peers were comfortable with various aspects of its implementation and "the importance of resembling the online courses with face-to-face classroom by utilizing videos" (p. 344).

Eskey and Schulte (2012) compared online student and faculty opinions about the content of courses and found that students desired extensive written feedback on assignments (with the exception of discussion board tasks) compared to faculty members' who taught commentary on discussion board assignments was most important and feedback on auto graded exams least valuable.

Drouin (2008) sought to understand if students' sense of connection with their instructor facilitated course satisfaction. However, Drouin noted that the feeling of association with the instructor did not correlate with course content retention. The positive effects of a linkage between online faculty member and students was supported in a study by Sebastianelli and Tamimi (2011) who found that online course activities that promoted instructor—learner dealings were the most valuable when teaching quantitative content.

Wagar and Carroll (2012) investigation of online group assignment grading strengthened the perceived need for close faculty–student connections. The outcomes of their research advocated that in addition to providing group members with anonymity when grading their colleagues' contributions to the group project, students believed that grading fairness improved with instructor participation.

The issue of how online faculty are prepared to teach online courses revealed several intriguing discoveries. In Schmidt et al. (2013) noted that "Most instructors new to online teaching begin with little to no training or preparation specific to this delivery model" (p. 13). One could extend their conclusion to online students who enroll in online courses believing that they will closely replicate the experience of face-to-face classes.

In addition to online faculty development training and managing student expectations for their online course experience, the limitations of the technology that makes online education possible must be considered. Vonderwell and Boboc (2013) warn that institutions must be mindful of students' connectivity options to avoid using the numerous technological features offered in Learning Management Systems (LMS) that could increase digital disparities between students.

3 Methodology

The survey instrument used to obtain data for this study was based on a Google Form and linked to the online course portal for convenience. Students were encouraged to participate in the survey as part of the faculty member's introduction letter. The survey consisted of six close-ended questions (five Likert scale 1 = little importance; 10 = high importance and one yes/no question) two open-ended questions and two background information questions. No course-related grade credit was offered for survey participation.

Replies to the six quantitative questions were analyzed in two ways; by course level = 300 (junior standing) and 400 (senior standing) and cumulative. Answers to the qualitative questions followed the same format (dividing the courses by class level) and in aggregate.

3.1 Research Questions of the Study

Six quantitative research questions were created to discover 300 and 400 level course participants' opinions towards interaction, feedback, and course design of online courses. They are presented below:

RQ 1 How much interaction do you desire with your faculty member?

RQ 2 Do you expect an online course to be similar to a face-to-face course?

RQ 3 To what extent do you find graded discussions helpful to learning in online courses?

RQ 4 To what degree do you value simplicity of design, content, and amount of interaction in an online course?

RQ 5 To what degree do you desire audio feedback on written assignments?

RQ 6 To what degree do supplemental videos and other internet web links enhance your online learning?

The research questions for the two qualitative questions were:

QUALR1 If only online faculty members knew this (fill in the blank) online courses be better.

QUALR2 What aggravates me most about online classes is?

Finally, two questions sought to determine how many online classes participants took prior to the class in which this survey was administered and the reasons participants took online classes.

3.2 Hypotheses for the Qualitative Questions in the Study

The hypotheses for the two qualitative questions were:

QUALR1o: There is no statistically significant difference between 300 and 400 level course participants' opinions regarding how online courses could be improved.

QUALR12o: There is no statistically significant difference between 300 and 400 level course participants' opinions regarding what aggravates them most about online classes.

4 Findings from the Study

Two general background information questions were posed in the survey to account for how many online classes class members took prior to enrolling in one of the courses taught by the researcher and in general why students enrolled in online classes at the University. The results for the background information questions of the participants are listed in Tables 1 and 2.

The findings to the six quantitative questions to discover 300 and 400 level course participants' opinions towards interaction, feedback, and course design of online courses are presented in Table 3.

A second goal of the study was to determine what if any differences existed between 300 and 400 course participants' opinions regarding interaction, feedback, and course design. The findings to the six quantitative questions segmented by 300 and 400 course participants' opinions towards interaction, feedback and course design of online courses are presented in aggregate in Table 4.

A third goal of the research project was to ascertain if there were general improvement suggestions to advance online course design. Two questions were asked of survey participants: QUALR1. If only online faculty members knew this (fill in the blank) online courses would be better and QUALR2. What aggravates me most about online classes is? The researcher grouped replies into seven categories to evaluate statistically the responses.

Table 1 Replies to background RQ 1. I take online courses for the following reason/s

Participant course level	Ease of access to course availability (%)	Speed—complete course quicker (%)	Less complicated than face-to-face courses (%)	Other (%)
300	50	12	3	34[a]
400	6	2	2	88[a]

[a]Principle replies for other were distance from campus and currently working full-time

Table 2 Replies to background RQ 2. How many online classes have you taken so far at EOU?

Participant course level	1	2	3	4	5	6+	Average
300	16	11	10	12	41	11	5
400	3	1	1	8	7	47	12
Total	19	12	11	20	48	58	8.5

Table 3 Aggregate replies to quantitative research questions[a]

RQ1		RQ2		RQ3		RQ4		RQ5		RQ6	
Interaction		Similarities		Graded discussion		Simplicity		Audio feedback		Supplemental sources	
Low	High	Low	High	Yes	No	Low	High	Low	High	Low	High
28	72	32	66	51	49	13	87	65	35	16	84

[a]*Note* Responses are expressed in percentages

Table 4 Cumulative replies to quantitative research questions segmented by 300 and 400 course participants[a]

	RQ1		RQ2		RQ3		RQ4		RQ5		RQ 6	
	Interaction with faculty member		Similarities		Graded discussion		Simplicity		Audio feedback		Supplemental sources	
	Low	High	Low	High	Yes	No	Low	High	Low	High	Low	High
300	79	21	22	62	48	52	85	15	26	74	20	80
400	35	65	13	87	54	46	11	89	45	55	13	87

[a]*Note* Responses are expressed in percentages

1. Complaints about faculty members' practices.
2. Group project problems.
3. Communication issues.
4. Expectations of faculty members are not clear.
5. Discussion problems.
6. Suggestions about faculty members' practices.
7. Other.

The aggregate responses to the two qualitative research questions are located in Tables 5 and 6.

Table 5 Replies to QUALR1. If only faculty members knew this (fill in the blank) online courses would be better

Category	300 level participants	400 level participants
Category 1	19	13
Category 2	8	1
Category 3	10	5
Category 4	4	1
Category 5	3	3
Category 6	40	24
Category 7	20	24
Total	104	71

The single greatest grumble from online students relates to faculty members' practices when conducting online classes

Table 6 Replies to QUALR2. What aggravates me most about online classes is?

Category	300 level participants	400 level participants
Category 1	24	19
Category 2	25	4
Category 3	11	13
Category 4	8	8
Category 5	18	5
Category 6	1	2
Category 7	17	20
Total	104	71

Three hundred level course participants complained nearly equally about faculty members' practices and group project problems while the top two grievances of 400 level course participants centered on a variety of issues in "Other" and faculty members' practices. Collectively criticisms (43) about faculty members' practices aggravated students the most of all categories.

The researcher used the Chi-Square method of data analysis to determine if statistically significant differences existed between the replies from 300 and 400 level course participants for Research Question 1. At a 0.05 level of significance, a critical point of 12.592 was obtained from the Chi-Square table. There were six degrees of freedom used in this study. The results are presented below in Table 7.

A Chi-Square value of 16.6465 was found which fell above the critical point of 12.592 needed at a 0.05 level of significance. Thus null hypothesis one was rejected indicating that there was a difference in how course level participants feel about their faculty members' online teaching practices.

The researcher used the Chi-Square method of data analysis to determine if statistically significant differences existed between the replies from 300 and 400 level course participants for Research Question 2. For null hypothesis two a 40.54821 Chi-Square value was found. It fell above the critical point at the 0.05 level of significance. Therefore, null hypothesis two was rejected and research hypothesis two was accepted. In terms of hypothesis two, there was a very significant difference in what aggravated 300 and 400 level course participants the most about online classes beyond the 0.005 % level (Table 8).

Table 7 QUALR1o: There is no statistically significant difference between 300 and 400 level course participants' opinions regarding how online courses could be improved

Hypothesis	Chi-Square (0.05 significance level)	Chi-Square results	p-value	Decision
1	12.592	16.6465	0.05	Reject the Null

Table 8 QUALR12o: There is no statistically significant difference between 300 and 400 level course participants' opinions regarding what aggravates them most about online classes

Hypothesis	Chi-Square (0.05 significance level)	Chi-Square results	p-value	Decision
2	12.592	40.54821	0.05	Reject the Null

5 Discussion of Results and Recommendations for Further Study

Result 1: There were notable differences between the preferences between 300 and 400 course level participants. The most important difference between 300 and 400 course level participants' was their motivation for taking online courses. 300 level students cited ease of access to courses for enrolling in online courses. 400 level students claimed online courses enabled them to continue to work full-time while pursuing their education.

Result 2: The average number of online courses taken by 300 level course participants was five (reflecting their progress and class standing in their degree program) while the average number of online courses taken by 400 level class participants' was 12 (also showing their tenure degree progress). Another factor for the variance between the average number of online courses taken between 300–400 level participants was the overwhelming (88 %) choice of 400 course participants of "Other" given for why they chose online courses. The two most commonly stated reasons for "Other" were distance from the campus (as the campus is located in a rural area of the state) and to enable 400 level participants to continue working while securing their business degree.

Result 3: A primary goal of this study was to determine what, if any, differences existed between 300 and 400 course participants' opinions regarding interaction, feedback, and course design. In total, the survey results demonstrated that course participants: (a) valued interaction with faculty, (b) valued supplemental course materials (e.g., videos, web links, etc.), (c) did not expect an online class to be similar to a face-to-face class, (d) were nearly split regarding the value of graded discussions, (d) valued simplicity of course design, content, and amount of interaction in online courses and (e) did not value audio feedback on written assignments. The findings indicate that both course level participants were in agreement regarding the properties and qualities of online course interaction, feedback, and design. The only difference between the two levels was the strength of their responses to the six quantitative questions.

Result 4: The third goal of this research project was to find out participants' specific complaints and suggested improvements about faculty members' practices and recommendations for course design improvements. Replies to the two qualitative research questions regarding course improvements and items that aggravate online students most point to the need for faculty improvements. The single greatest objection from 300 and 400 online course level students related to faculty members' practices when conducting online classes. This conclusion was verified statistically. Regarding the second research question, which inquired about what components of online courses aggravated 300 and 400 course participants the most, the number one complaint shared by the two course levels that faculty members' practices (eg., poor course planning, response to inquiries, assignment details, etc.). However, in general, the two course levels differed on their rankings of what elements of online course qualities aggravated them the most as confirmed by the results of the Chi-Square test indicting a significance result at the 0.005 level.

6 Recommendations

There are four recommendations offered as a result of this study.

The first is to enlarge the subject population of a future study (obviously the population size of this research is too small to make generalized conclusions) and include all course levels. Additionally, it would be valuable to consider comparing responses of undergraduate and graduate course levels to discern if any statistically significant differences exist between these age and experience level students. The second recommendation is to encourage surveys such as the one used in this investigation to be utilized on a regular basis by each major in a business program to create baseline measurements and use the results to monitor trends and benchmark for improvements. The third recommendation is create a parallel survey for face-to-face courses (separate from end of course student evaluations) to compare the results with online courses. The comparisons could reveal what if any trends may exist on a macro-level regarding a College of Business' course design, faculty performance, and other elements that are indicative of overall effectiveness. The fourth recommendation is to utilize data from surveys such as the one used in this inquiry as regular discussion points for faculty members. Too frequently, faculty do not have credible data to base deliberations regarding changes that may be needed to not merely to "satisfy complaints" but rather provide ongoing improvement reports to various university and accreditation agencies' requirements and setting new standards of excellence and fulfillment of mission statement commitments.

Acknowledgements The author wishes to thank Dr. Allen Klingenberg, Ms. Nerea Delgado Fernández and Ms. Mary Mutua for their roles in the statistical analysis in this paper.

References

All HarvardX Offerings (All time) (2015). Retrieved from http://harvardx.harvard.edu/harvardx-insights/world-map-enrollment

Changing course: Ten years of tracking online education in the United States (2012). Retrieved from http://onlinelearningconsortium.org/survey_report/changing-course-ten-years-tracking-online-education-united-states/

Drouin M (2008) The relationship between students' perceived sense of community and satisfaction, achievement and retention in an online course. Q. Rev. Distance Educ. 9:3

Eskey M, Schulte M (2012) Comparing attitudes of online instructors and online college students: quantitative results for training, evaluation and administration. Online J. Distance Learn. Adm. 15:5

Schmidt SW, Hodge EM, Tschida CM (2013) How university faculty members developed their online teaching skills. Q. Rev. Distance Educ. 14(3):131–140

Sebastianelli R, Tamimi N (2011) Business statistics and management science online: teaching strategies and assessment of student learning. J. Educ. Bus. 86(6):317–325. doi:10.1080/08832323.2010.525545

Sun Q, Ganesh G (2014) Developing and teaching an online MBA marketing research class: implications for online learning effectiveness. J. Educ. Bus. 89(7):337–345. doi:10.1080/08832323.2013.806885

Vonderwell S, Boboc M (2013) Promoting formative assessment in online teaching and learning. Techtrends: Linking Res. Pract. Improv. Learn. 57(4):22–27. doi:10.1007/s11528-013-0673-x

Wagar TH, Carroll WR (2012) Examining student preferences of group work evaluation approaches: evidence from business management undergraduate students. J. Educ. Bus. 87 (6):358–362. doi:10.1080/08832323.2011.628345

MIX
Papier aus verantwortungsvollen Quellen
Paper from responsible sources
FSC® C105338

If you have any concerns about our products,
you can contact us on
ProductSafety@springernature.com

In case Publisher is established outside the EU,
the EU authorized representative is:
Springer Nature Customer Service Center GmbH
Europaplatz 3, 69115 Heidelberg, Germany

Printed by Libri Plureos GmbH
in Hamburg, Germany